HISTORIC INDIANAPOLIS
FIRES & DISASTERS

JACK FINNEY

THE
History
PRESS

Published by The History Press
Charleston, SC
www.historypress.com

The Bowen Merrill fire. *Indiana Historical Society, P0411.*

First published 2024

Manufactured in the United States

ISBN 9781467155052

Library of Congress Control Number: 2023946757

For Lesley.
"Never, My Love"

CONTENTS

PREFACE

There are two types of disasters: natural and human made. And Indianapolis has dealt with both types in its more than two-hundred-year history.

Human beings can't control natural disasters. However, with modern technology, some natural disasters, like storms, can be predicted. And by anticipating them, we can prepare for them.

Scientists can also predict that other natural disasters, such as earthquakes, will happen but can't tell *when* they will occur. All we can do is prepare for them, knowing they are coming—someday. For example, we can build structures designed to withstand earthquakes, hurricanes or even tsunamis. But in the end, we can't control nature itself.

On the other hand, human-made disasters are controllable. By their very nature, these disasters are caused by a mistake someone has made. It's often something small, seemingly inconsequential at the time, that quickly goes out of control. Of course, if no one made mistakes, there would be no human-made disasters. But that's just not possible. No one is perfect. Everyone makes mistakes; it's a simple fact of life. Luckily, most mistakes don't affect anyone other than the person who makes them. However, other errors become huge and sometimes cost people their lives.

Indianapolis and Marion County have had their share of both types of disasters. That's the subject of this book. Most of the catastrophes I've written about are human made. That's not to say the area hasn't suffered from natural disasters. In fact, very few types of natural disasters have *not* happened in Marion County within the last two hundred years. For example, there have been no volcanos, no major landslides, no avalanches, no tsunamis, no hurricanes (although we've had remnants of hurricanes bring wind and rain to the area).

But I haven't chronicled every disaster in Marion County during the nineteenth and early twentieth centuries. For instance, I didn't write about the various epidemics that threatened Indianapolis.

The town's first catastrophe was an epidemic that occurred soon after its founding. The summer of 1821 found the then-small village of Indianapolis struck by an unknown disease. It was so threatening that there was talk of abandoning the town. That never happened, but about twenty-five people, mostly children, in a population of just a few hundred people died. Today, it's believed that the unknown disease was probably malaria.

Various diseases always threatened Indianapolis's citizens, sometimes reaching epidemic levels. Cholera was one example. It reached epidemic levels in 1832, 1849, 1866 and 1878–79 but was a constant menace. In addition, smallpox, malaria, tuberculosis and many other diseases were ongoing risks in the nineteenth and early twentieth centuries.

Another major health threat was the influenza pandemic of 1918. It had a massive impact on the world and Indianapolis. World War I raged from 1914 to 1918 and killed an estimated 15 to 30 million military personnel and civilians. While that number is enormous, the flu, in 1918 alone, killed a staggering 50 million people worldwide. I didn't write about this disease, although it was responsible for the deaths of over 1,600 Indianapolis citizens.

You won't find a chapter about the 1913 floods, which caused deaths and widespread property damage in Indianapolis and elsewhere. There are other books about this flood, and I couldn't add anything to what has already been written.

But I hope you will like reading about the catastrophes that I *did* write about. Since they occurred over one hundred years ago, most of these incidents are little remembered today. However, some of you may be aware of a few of them. If you are, after reading this book, I hope it will reveal something about them you hadn't known before. Most of all, I hope everyone will enjoy reading this book as much as I liked researching and writing it.

Note: Anywhere I've mentioned a dollar amount, I've also included an amount in parentheses. That's the modern equivalent adjusted for inflation. It was calculated separately according to each incident's date and dollar amount. For instance, $1 in 1860 is equivalent to $36.37 in 2023, while that same dollar in 1910 has a 2023 value of $31.77.

Also, Indianapolis gave street names to some downtown alleys. There are many theories as to why they did this. I won't attempt an explanation here, but it can confuse things. For instance, if Pearl or Scioto Street is mentioned, you might picture grand thoroughfares when they're actually just narrow alleys.

ACKNOWLEDGEMENTS

My thanks go to several individuals and organizations. They are, in no particular order:

my wife, my daughter, my son and their families
Indianapolis Firefighters Museum
Indiana State Library
Indiana Historical Society
Hoosier State Chronicles
NewspaperArchive.com
Newspapers.com
Indiana.railfan.net
Avon-Washington Township Public Library
Plainfield-Guilford Township Public Library
Allen Knight
Greg Roembke
Jim Williamson
David Lewis
Brian Killilea
Kristen Christiansen

But most of all, I'd like to thank Rodger Birchfield, who was a good friend for almost fifty years. Rodger was also my mentor as I studied the history of the Indianapolis Fire Department. I wish he could've been here to see this book.

1

TWO ACCIDENTS IN ONE DAY

When Indianapolis was founded in 1821, it was surrounded by a heavily wooded wilderness. Gradually, a few roads—often little more than foot trails—were hacked through these woods, connecting the small town to other towns. Finally, the National Road (now U.S. 40) reached Indianapolis in 1830, but travel was still slow. For instance, a stagecoach trip from Indianapolis to the southern Indiana town of Madison took three and a half days in 1826. The stage left Indianapolis at 7:00 a.m. on Thursday and finally arrived in Madison at 5:00 p.m. on Sunday after three overnight stops. That same trip today in an automobile on modern roads takes less than two hours.

So, Indianapolis citizens had reason to celebrate when the first railroad, the Madison and Indianapolis Railroad, reached their town on October 1, 1847. Travel would now be much quicker. But faster travel sometimes comes at the cost of personal safety. Newspapers of the day were full of stories about accidents on various railroads across the country, often involving fatalities.

By 1852, Indianapolis had several railroads converging on it from all directions. The area had been lucky, because there had been no fatal railroad accidents in Marion County in the five years since the first railroad had come to town. But unfortunately, that enviable record was broken twice in one day on Christmas Eve 1852.

In December 1852, heavy rains caused flooding throughout central Indiana. As a result, some small streams in Marion County temporarily became raging rivers. This rushing water damaged supports under several bridges but two in particular: the bridge for the Madison and Indianapolis

Railroad over Pleasant Run and one of the bridges for the Lafayette and Indianapolis Railroad over Crooked Creek.

Both bridges collapsed when trains tried to cross them on December 24, 1852. But unfortunately, newspapers gave scant information concerning these accidents. The only information about them appeared in two articles printed in the December 25, 1852 edition of the *Indianapolis Daily State Sentinel*. The articles clarified that these were two separate accidents on different railroads and described them as having occurred "yesterday morning."

The Lafayette and Indianapolis Railroad ran northwest out of Indianapolis. In later years, its route changed, but it's thought that in 1852, there were four places the railroad crossed over Crooked Creek. The first crossing was a little east of 3400 North Cold Springs Road. Another was in the vicinity of approximately 4000 North Cooper Road. There was a crossing at about 2600 West Forty-Second Street, and the fourth was a little northwest of the intersection of Forty-Sixth Street and Cooper Road. All of those descriptions use modern road names and addresses. In 1852, there weren't many roads in those areas, and there were no addresses. Since none of the newspaper articles specified which bridge over Crooked Creek collapsed, we are left to wonder exactly where the incident occurred. The only clue was in the *Indianapolis Daily State Sentinel* article that said the accident occurred "five miles from this city." That might suggest that it was the crossing northwest of Forty-Sixth Street and Cooper Road that collapsed, but there is no way to confirm this.

What is known is that a freight train left Indianapolis going northwest to Lafayette but never made it. As the train crossed one of the bridges over Crooked Creek, the bridge supports, weakened by the rushing water, gave way, and the locomotive plunged into the stream. The train's engineer and fireman both escaped without any injuries. Unfortunately, another man wasn't as lucky. The article in the December 25, 1852 edition of the *Indianapolis Daily State Sentinel* described the victim as "a man in front of the foremost car." Remember, this was a freight train, so there wouldn't have been any passengers. This man—presumably a railroad employee— panicked because of the accident and jumped into the water, apparently in an attempt to escape the wreckage. However, the swift current in the usually calm stream quickly swept him underneath the locomotive as it lay in the water. The man was trapped there and drowned. The newspaper never gave the name of the unfortunate victim.

A passenger train traveling behind the freight train on the same track was able to stop in time, preventing it from crashing into the partially derailed freight train. Even though the passenger train had stopped successfully, it couldn't return to Indianapolis for reasons that weren't clear. According to the same edition of the *Indianapolis Daily State Sentinel*, the passengers and their luggage were carried back to town in horse-drawn wagons.

The other crash occurred in almost exactly the same way—just in a different location. This time, the rushing water in Pleasant Run had washed away the supports for the Madison and Indianapolis Railroad bridge. A freight train bound for Madison, Indiana, left the station but made it only about a mile and a half outside the Indianapolis city limits. In that era, the southern city limit was South Street. As the train crossed over Pleasant Run, the bridge gave way.

As the bridge fell, the locomotive and six other freight cars dropped about twenty feet into the stream. Ten other cars remained on the tracks and were not damaged. The engineer, Henry Johnson; the fireman (whose name was not given in the article); and Horace Bacon, another crewman, were all missing after the crash and presumed dead. The damage was extensive, with the December 25, 1852 edition of the *Indianapolis Daily State Sentinel* reporting, "The wreck presents a horrid appearance." The body of the fireman was recovered later that same day. Mr. Bacon's body was found on Christmas Day in the water underneath the wreckage. However, the engineer's body could not be located. That led to a rather odd turn of events—if they are proven to be true.

This author first learned of these two accidents while researching a later railroad accident. In an article in the February 2, 1884 edition of the *Indianapolis News*, there was a mention of these two older incidents. That article also told of how the engineer's body in the Pleasant Run crash was missing for several years. Allegedly, it was finally located when another flood washed away a sandbar in the stream and exposed his remains. Sadly, the body had remained in the vicinity of the accident scene covered by sand. The article continued, saying that G.W. Allred, the Sexton of Greenlawn Cemetery, had not given the unfortunate engineer's remains a proper burial. Instead, he kept them in a box in his office at the cemetery as a curiosity.

This author searched newspapers published between 1853 and 1870, looking for articles about when the body was found, the circumstances of the discovery, et cetera. However, nothing could be found aside from the one article printed in 1884.

The author did find notices in several newspapers confirming that the engineer's body was missing after the accident. For instance, the January 6, 1853 edition of the *Indianapolis Weekly State Sentinel* contained a notice. It said that Mr. Cravens, the vice-president of the Madison and Indianapolis Railroad, stated that a handsome reward was available for the recovery of the body of Henry Johnson, the engineer of the ill-fated train. It then described Mr. Johnson as having been five feet, nine inches tall and heavyset, with light hair and blue eyes. It said that at the time of the incident, he had a small amount of money in his pocket, along with a gold watch and chain. This same notice appeared in several papers around the state. That was almost two weeks after the accident.

This author also found confirmation that Garrison W. Allred had been the sexton of Greenlawn Cemetery in Indianapolis from 1860 to 1869. (A sexton is the person in charge of a cemetery.) Following this, he became the Marion County coroner but held this position for only one year. This information came from various Indianapolis city directories.

So, some parts of the story are definitely true. Mr. Johnson's body was missing following the accident. This author also found that G.W. Allred had been the sexton of Greenlawn Cemetery for several years. His term of office (in those days, the Indianapolis City Council appointed the sexton) started about seven years after the railroad accident.

However, there is no confirmation for three parts of the story. First, how long did Henry Johnson's body remain lost? Second, was it ever actually found? And third—and the most intriguing part of the story—if the engineer's body was recovered, did G.W. Allred really keep the poor man's bones in a box in his office, displaying them as a macabre souvenir?

But something else might have happened to the body. Pleasant Run empties into the much larger White River, about a mile and a half downstream from the accident site. Could Mr. Johnson's body have been swept downstream into the river following the accident? If that were the case, his body might never have been located. Or it could have been found much farther downriver and never correctly identified. Whatever the answer, the final location of Henry Johnson's remains is not known. Hopefully, they finally received a proper burial sometime in the intervening years.

Today, there is still a railroad bridge over Pleasant Run where this accident occurred. It's on the west side of Garfield Park, just a little southwest of the intersection of East Pleasant Run Parkway, North Drive and Pagoda Drive.

2

DEATH AT THE STATE FAIRGROUNDS IN THE 1860s

Unfortunately, many people associate the Indiana State Fairgrounds with disaster and death. Although it is primarily a place for fun and laughter, people also remember the tragic explosion that took the lives of seventy-four spectators during an ice skating show on the evening of Halloween 1963. Fresher still in many minds is the stage collapse that occurred on August 11, 2011, and resulted in seven deaths. Both of these unfortunate incidents occurred at the current Indiana State Fairgrounds.

But sadly, if you go back to the nineteenth century and a different Indiana State Fairgrounds site, you will find that disaster and death were also associated with that location.

The very first Indiana State Fair ran from October 19 to October 22, 1852. That inaugural event took place in Indianapolis at what later became Military Park. That park is still located at the southwest corner of New York and West Streets. The following year, the fair moved to Lafayette, and in 1854, it moved to Madison. From 1855 to 1858, the state fair was held back at Military Park in Indianapolis. Then in 1859, the fair moved again to New Albany.

But in early 1860 came news that the fair had found a new permanent home. The fair board spent $14,400 ($517,029) to purchase the property as a new home for its annual event. The new fairgrounds comprised about thirty-six acres in a rural locale just north of Indianapolis. The main entrance to the fairgrounds was located near what later became Nineteenth and Alabama Streets.

The fair board chose this location because it felt it was far enough away from the city that it wouldn't interfere with the daily lives of Indianapolis residents. Despite this seemingly rural setting, Indianapolis soon grew to encompass the site. By the 1870s, the fairgrounds were inside the Indianapolis city limits.

Today, this tract of land is part of the Herron-Morton Place neighborhood. The fairgrounds property was bounded by what is now Nineteenth Street to the south, Twenty-Second Street to the north, Talbott Street to the west and Central Avenue to the east.

Unfortunately, this relatively small plot of land would become very familiar with death. Over 1,700 people would lose their lives within these thirty-six acres between early 1862 and late 1869.

The 1860 state fair took place at its new location in Indianapolis. The ninth annual Indiana State Fair opened on October 22, 1860, to great fanfare. But civil unrest was looming on the horizon, and in April 1861, the American Civil War began.

A few days after the war started, Indiana governor Oliver Morton sent a telegram to President Abraham Lincoln, offering to raise and equip ten thousand troops. Naturally, the state needed somewhere to train all these men, so the new fairgrounds became an army camp. The facility was named Camp Morton in honor of the governor.

In early 1862, the camp's mission changed, and it became a prisoner of war facility. A wooden palisade was erected, enclosing much of the former fairgrounds. This high fence had a walkway around its perimeter near the top for armed soldiers to guard prisoners. The camp was designed to hold about 3,000 prisoners, but from the beginning, it was overcrowded. By the end of its first week, it held almost 3,700 men. It reached its peak population, nearly 5,000 prisoners, in the summer of 1864.

The camp had several other problems besides overcrowding; among them were meager rations, a lack of warm clothing, inadequate medical care and disease. In addition, many prisoners from the Deep South had never experienced the bitterly cold weather of an Indiana winter. This fact, coupled with the other problems, caused the deaths of more than 1,700 prisoners. The exact number of deaths is not known. In addition, 7 POWs died during escape attempts and fights in the camp. All these men were buried in a special section of Greenlawn Cemetery in Indianapolis. A wooden board with a number painted on it marked each grave. Prison officials compiled a list containing each soldier's name, rank and home state. Every name on the list had a number corresponding to the number on a grave marker to identify the man buried there. Unfortunately, this list was destroyed by a fire in the cemetery's office a few years after the end of the war. After the war, some families had their loved ones' remains exhumed and returned for burial closer to their homes. That still left over 1,600 men buried at Greenlawn. As the decades passed, with the loss of the list and the wooden identification boards becoming weathered and illegible, the names of the soldiers buried in these graves were no longer known.

In 1933, the Confederate dead were disinterred and reburied in a mass grave at Crown Hill Cemetery in Indianapolis. That grave was marked with a six-foot-tall granite monument. Then in the late 1980s, extensive research was begun to compile a list of the possible names of the men buried in the mass grave. As a result, ten smaller monuments with brass plaques listing the names of all those believed to have been buried there were placed at the site in 1991.

Prisoners of war were not the only people who died on the grounds of Camp Morton. The U.S. Army executed at least four men at the camp. First, on March 27, 1863, Private Robert Gay of the Seventy-First Indiana Regiment was shot by a firing squad. He'd been charged with desertion. Then in 1864, another military firing squad executed three "bounty jumpers." A "bounty jumper" was a man who'd been paid, usually $300 ($5,694), to take another man's place in the army. The "jumper" would enlist and then desert, often going to a different city to do the same thing.

After the Civil War ended, the camp's property reverted to the fair board. The federal government paid the board almost $10,000 ($182,828) to compensate them for using the land and for damage caused to the property.

The 1861 Indiana State Fair was canceled because of the war. But surprisingly, the fair was still held in 1862, 1863 and 1864, despite the ongoing war. With the fairgrounds being used as a POW camp, the state fair was again held at Military Park in those years.

Although the Civil War ended in April 1865 and officials released the last prisoners from Camp Morton in June 1865, that year's fair was held in Fort Wayne. Possibly, there wasn't enough time to prepare the regular fairgrounds for the annual state fair, which was held in October. However, in 1866, the fair returned to its traditional home at what had formerly been Camp Morton.

By 1869, people were looking forward to that year's fair and all the fun they would have there. A letter published in the September 13, 1869 edition of *Terre Haute's Daily Wabash Express* newspaper and many other newspapers across the state told of all the new attractions that would be seen at the upcoming event. The letter, signed by the president and secretary of the fair board, was addressed to "Farmers, Mechanics, Manufacturers, and People of the State of Indiana." It also pointed out that fares for a railroad trip to the fair in Indianapolis were at half price during the event. Finally, the letter urged: "Come early. Bring your wives and children. Young men, bring your sweethearts. You will all find something to interest you."

The 1869 edition of the fair began on September 27 and was well attended. By October 1, the *Indianapolis Daily Sentinel* reported, "Visitors to the state fair looked in vain for a first-class hotel." However, not everything was fun and games. The same newspaper reported that a lady visiting from Miami County had a purse containing $30 ($657) stolen while she attended the fair.

Friday, October 1, 1869, began as a sunny day. Estimates for attendance that day ranged from twenty thousand to thirty thousand. As promised, there was much to see and do at the fair. There were exhibits of everything from farm implements to fine art. A glimpse into the future was also on display as John Smith, "the Hoosier Aeronaut," made a balloon ascension into the sky above the fairgrounds. Many families brought picnic lunches to enjoy. And for those who didn't come prepared, a wide variety of food was available at the many concessions stands.

Among the many activities were demonstrations of steam sawmills built by various companies. Steam power was a new and exciting technology in those times. One of the exhibitors was the Western Machine Works of Indianapolis, a machine shop located at 125 South Pennsylvania Street. The company, owned by Edward Sinker and his partners Daniel Yandes and his son, George Yandes, was founded in 1850 and was well known locally and nationally. It built steam engines and steam-powered saws.

On the afternoon of Friday, October 1, several sawmill companies held a competition to see which of their saws could cut the most wood in a given amount of time. Of course, each manufacturer wanted to prove their saw was the best. The Western Machine Works sawmill won the contest.

The race was already over when, at around 3:00 p.m., one of the Western Machine Works company representatives decided to cut up the remaining wood that was left over from the competition. He was almost finished when he paused the saw to clear away the sawdust that had accumulated around the blade.

The steam engine had stopped, but the boiler was still building pressure when it suddenly exploded with an earthshaking roar. The boiler was constructed using quarter-inch-thick iron. As it blew apart, this became lethal shrapnel, with shards of the metal flying in every direction. In addition, parts of the saw's machinery were torn apart. Jagged pieces slashed through the crowd of spectators with devastating results.

One part of the sawmill weighing almost four hundred pounds flew into the air and came crashing down through the roof of a nearby animal shed. It landed in a pen that held a prize-winning bull. The bull was unharmed, except the tip of one of its horns was broken off by the metal. Other animals weren't so lucky. There were at least three horses killed, including one that was pulling a carriage carrying a man, his wife and their young daughter. The force of the explosion also caused the carriage to be overturned, throwing the family onto the ground. Luckily, they were unharmed. One part of the sawmill, estimated to weigh over one thousand pounds, was propelled three hundred feet away from its original location.

Indiana's Governor Conrad Baker was in attendance that day. A large piece of metal barely missed him but hit his coachman, who was standing nearby. The coachman, Henry Coleman, was seriously injured, suffering a broken skull. He eventually recovered.

Also among the visitors that day were two hundred students from Asbury College (later DePauw University) in Greencastle, Indiana. One of them, John A. McVey, was seriously injured. His father, John F. McVey, was also at the fair that day. After the explosion, he helped load some injured persons into a wagon. He then rode with them to the Surgical Institute, a hospital in Indianapolis, to assist with unloading them. After returning to the fair, he learned that his son had been injured and taken to the Surgical Institute. Mr. McVey then returned to the institute and began asking about his son. One of the victims who was lying nearby recognized Mr. McVey's voice and said weakly, "Here I am, Father." It turned out that the boy had been one of the victims John F. McVey had assisted earlier. Unfortunately, the young McVey had been so disfigured due to extensive injuries that his own father hadn't recognized him. Sadly, he died two days later. Another young man named Myron McVey died at the scene. There were conflicting reports about whether he was a brother or cousin of John A. McVey.

Edward Sinker, one of the partners of the Western Machine Works, had just walked away from the sawmill when the explosion occurred. He was standing nearby, talking with his wife. They were both badly injured but survived.

In an interview published in the *Indianapolis Journal* on October 2, 1869, Mr. Sinker stated that one common cause of such an explosion was putting cold water into a hot boiler. However, he did not think that was the cause of this incident, as he'd checked the water gauge just minutes before the explosion. He said it showed there was sufficient water in the boiler, so no water needed to be added. These types of steam engines usually ran at 80 to 100 pounds of pressure. When Mr. Sinker last checked, the steam gauge on the boiler showed 120 pounds of pressure. However, since the boiler was rated to stand up to 160 pounds, he did not feel this pressure was excessive. He also stated that the sawmill his company exhibited the previous year had "carried a heavier head of steam."

The man running the engine, John Goll, and two of his assistants, Jerome Spriggs and Henry Costin, were all killed in the blast. Phanuel L. Davis, the superintendent of the Power Hall, was also killed, as were two other men employed by other sawmill companies. The other victims were spectators who were looking for a day of fun at the fair.

The newspapers of that time published very graphic details about the condition of the bodies of the dead and injured. Many victims suffered traumatic amputations, steam burns and other horrible injuries. One lurid newspaper headline read, "Humanity Mangled, Roasted, Scalded, and Burned." Another said: "Fragments of Bodies Scattered in All Directions."

As news of the explosion spread through Indianapolis, a sort of panic ensued. Almost every citizen seemed to have had a relative or friend who was at the fair that day. They were anxious to learn whether their loved ones or acquaintances were victims. Wild rumors also spread throughout the town. Some people claimed that one hundred people or more had been killed. Luckily, that was untrue, but the number of deaths and injuries was still difficult for many people to comprehend.

In those days, there were no ambulances. Instead, private carriages and wagons were used to transport the injured and the dead. There was controversy when a few wagon owners attempted to charge money before taking injured persons to the hospital.

Morbid crowds flooded the street in front of the Surgical Institute. That facility was a private hospital on the northeast corner of Illinois and Georgia Streets, where many victims received treatment. As wagons brought in the injured people, the crowd pushed forward to get a glimpse of the victim to see if they were someone they knew. Other people with similar intentions crowded around the entrance to William Weaver's undertaking establishment at 39 North Illinois Street, where the dead were taken.

Newspapers gave figures ranging between twelve and thirty persons killed outright, with more than sixty reportedly injured. Some of those who were reportedly injured died later. For example, a report in the *Indianapolis Journal* on October 2, 1869, said that a man—not identified in the newspaper—

died at the Jeffersonville, Madison and Indianapolis Railroad Station on South Street. The man, who had been injured in the explosion earlier that day, was waiting for a train to take him home.

The *Indianapolis Daily State Sentinel*, reporting on October 4, three days after the explosion, listed twenty fatalities. Four of these victims were still unidentified at that time. Of these identified victims, ten were from Indianapolis or Marion County. The remaining identified victims were one person each from Morgan, Johnson, Clark, Hamilton, Scott and Allen Counties. Two victims, who died a few days later, were both from Hendricks County. The same newspaper also said, "There were probably a number of others who were injured slightly, in one way or another. But there are at least forty persons whose injuries are severe and of whom several, although improving, are still in danger."

It was hard to obtain an accurate count of the victims. Some of the dead and injured had been taken away by friends immediately following the explosion. These victims were all removed from the fairgrounds before anyone could record their names. Therefore, they may have never appeared on any lists of injured or dead victims.

Only one child died in this incident. She was two-and-a-half-year-old Clara Dawson, the daughter of Mr. and Mrs. Henry Dawson of Marion County. The child was struck in the head by a piece of debris and died a few minutes later. Despite the youngster's death, the *Indianapolis Daily State Sentinel* on October 4, 1882, made an outlandish observation. Its article said, "Among the dead, there have been no children, and the theory has been advanced that such (i.e., any children) may have been blown entirely to pieces." Fortunately, no children were reported missing.

Coroner Garrison Allred empaneled a jury to investigate the incident. The jury, which consisted of a medical doctor and five other citizens, made their findings known on October 5. At that time, there were twenty-one known deaths. Their verdict read: "The 21 victims all came to their deaths from injuries received by the explosion of a boiler attached to one of E.T. Sinker & Companies portable steam engines, at the Indiana State Fairgrounds, on the first day of October 1869. Further, that the explosion was caused by the carelessness and culpable mismanagement on the part of the engineer in charge, John Goll, who is deceased."

Officials never gave the total number of deaths. However, two other victims died from their injuries in the following weeks, making the death toll at least twenty-three. Some modern sources give the number as thirty or almost thirty.

In the year following the disaster, several people sued Sinker and Company for their injuries or the death of a loved one. Despite the coroner's verdict, which ruled that an employee of Sinker and Company was responsible for the explosion, the courts always sided with the company. As a result, none of the lawsuits were successful.

Edward Sinker, one of the owners of the Western Machine Works, died on April 5, 1871. That was just a year and a half after the explosion seriously injured him. However, it was not believed that his death was the result of the injuries he'd suffered. After his death, his widow sold the company, and it became the Sinker-Davis Company. The business continued under that name until the early 1960s.

The Indiana State Fair continued to be held annually at this location until 1891. It then moved to its present location at East Thirty-Eighth Street and Fall Creek Parkway.

The former fairgrounds property was sold in 1891 to three Indianapolis businessmen for $275,100 ($9,009,072). They tore down all the fair buildings, including the large Exposition Hall, which had been built for $100,000 ($2,483,417) in 1873. At 300 feet long and 150 feet wide, this majestic two-story brick building was one of the architectural showpieces of Indianapolis in that era.

After clearing the former fairgrounds, streets and sidewalks were added, and several hundred building lots were laid out and sold. In a nod to the land's usage during the Civil War, the new neighborhood was named Morton Place. It soon became the place for Indianapolis's well-to-do citizens to build their homes.

Today, the area, in combination with another historic area just to the south, is known as the Herron-Morton Place Neighborhood. It is a thriving community of mostly older, large, two-story homes. It was placed in the National Register of Historic Places in 1983.

Several markers now commemorate the area's previous usage as a POW camp. However, none mention that it was also the site of the Indiana State Fair in 1860 and from 1866 to 1891. Small commemorative plaques were placed at the four street corners that mark the camp's boundaries. On North Alabama Street, between Nineteenth and Twentieth Streets, is a historical marker to remember Camp Morton. And as mentioned earlier, tribute is paid to the POWs reburied at Crown Hill. However, there is no memorial remembering the many people who died due to the steam engine explosion during the 1869 Indiana State Fair.

3

THE MORRISON OPERA HOUSE FIRE

This chapter is unique because it's about an Indianapolis catastrophe that didn't happen. That's not to say that nothing took place. There was still a major fire—a fire that destroyed two large, multistory buildings and put hundreds of people in danger. But no lives were lost. As you will read, the credit for preventing these deaths goes almost entirely to one man. He was a true hero—one who has remained unheralded in Indianapolis history until now.

The Morrison Opera House Fire, which occurred on January 17, 1870, had the potential to be one of the worst tragedies in Indianapolis's history. Everything needed to produce a horrific loss of life was in place. Consider these facts:

A. There was an audience of several hundred people in the auditorium.
B. The auditorium was on the third floor of the building.
C. The only entrance/exit for the auditorium was by one narrow stairway, which went from the first to the third floor with no landing in between.
D. Once on the first floor, there were only two exit doors from the building.

Yes, everything needed to bring about a tragic disaster was in place, except for one final ingredient: panic.

The Morrison Opera House had been open since September 1866. In its relatively short lifetime, it hosted many concerts, plays and other events. However, it was a lecture about the dangers of excessive alcohol consumption that drew an audience of over three hundred on January 17, 1870. The speaker on that fateful evening was John Bartholomew Gough, a well-known temperance lecturer. Mr. Gough kept his audience enthralled and entertained, which is what he was famous for.

Then at a little after 9:00 p.m., one of the audience members, Reverend James Crawford, the minister of Trinity Methodist Church in Indianapolis, happened to glance down. As he did, he thought he spied a slight hint of smoke seeping between the seams of the wooden floor at his feet. Investigating further, he leaned down and felt the floor—it was hot. That confirmed his fears that the building was on fire. He whispered to his family, who was seated with him, to leave the building. He then went to the people sitting nearest the exit and quietly asked them to begin leaving. He urged them to move slowly and avoid drawing too much attention. He went from row to row, calmly and deliberately clearing out the audience without causing any panic. There was a slight hint of excitement as the audience filed out, but no one ran, no one tried to push ahead of others and, most importantly, no one yelled, "Fire!" In this way, Reverend Crawford safely evacuated the entire auditorium.

The January 18, 1870 *Indianapolis News* said, "Had the alarm been given at once, before the audience had time to think, a panic would have ensued, the consequences of which would have been frightful beyond conception!" The same article also praised Reverend Crawford, saying, "The manner in which the hall was cleared was truly wonderful, and Mr. Crawford deserves the greatest credit for his presence of mind, to which, alone, many persons owe their lives today."

The Morrison Opera House was made of brick, four stories tall and about ninety by two hundred feet. It was located on the northeast corner of Meridian and Maryland Streets. The building was divided into three two-story bays used for retail establishments. Above that, the entire third floor comprised the opera hall. The fourth floor held the balcony for the opera hall. That fourth-floor balcony extended for about a third of the length of the opera hall. The rest of the fourth floor was open from its ceiling to the third floor below. Luckily, the balcony was not in use that fateful evening. Otherwise, it's very likely that safely evacuating people from there would have been much more difficult.

The south retail bay was vacant. Its recent tenant, Murphy, Johnson and Company, a wholesale dry goods company, had moved to its new location across the street on the southeast corner of Meridian and Maryland Streets. The middle bay's occupant was Alford, Talbot and Company, a wholesale

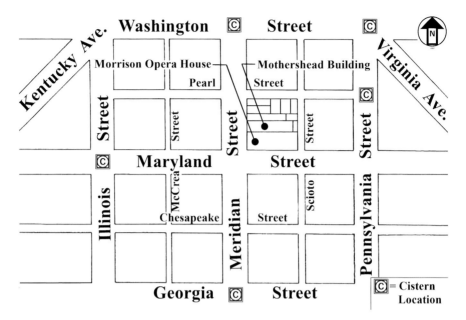

A map showing the cisterns near the Morrison Opera House in 1870. The following year and beyond, hydrants were available in many more locations than cisterns were. *Map by author.*

grocery firm. The auditorium's ticket office used part of its second-floor space. Patterson, Moore and Talbott, a wholesale drug company, occupied the north bay. Two companies of the Indiana National Guard also had room to store their equipment in the building and used the auditorium as their meeting hall.

This fire occurred before Indianapolis had any type of community water supply. Ironically, the city would sign a contract later this same month to build a municipal waterworks. By December 1871, Indianapolis would have several miles of water mains and two hundred hydrants for firefighting.

But this fire occurred in January 1870. There were *no* water mains and *no* hydrants. The only water available for fighting this fire came from cisterns. The city had begun building cisterns in 1852, and by 1870, there were seventy-eight of them, with most located in the downtown, high-value area.

Cisterns were usually located at or near street intersections so that they would be accessible to fire apparatus approaching from any direction. They were underground reservoirs that held anywhere from a few thousand to sixty thousand gallons of water or more. Firefighters accessed them through a manhole cover in the street. A pumper would use its hard suction hose to draft the water for firefighting. The drivers of the steam fire engines knew the location of cisterns, just as today's engine chauffeurs know hydrant locations.

On that cold January evening, all three of IFD's steamers drafted from cisterns for their water supply. Fortunately, these cisterns had enough water to extinguish this fire—but just barely.

After extinguishing the fire, it was discovered that the firefighting had almost entirely emptied the water in all three cisterns. Other cisterns could have been used, but that would have necessitated moving the steam fire engines and making longer hose lays. That would have delayed the firefighting. So, ultimately, the other cisterns weren't needed—this time.

Newspapers of the day pointed out how inadequate cisterns were. The January 18, 1870 edition of the *Indianapolis News* commented, "The small supply of water, obtainable last night, is conclusive proof of the need for a waterworks here." The paper also reported that the following day, one of the steamers was playing water over the ruins of the fire while the other

This photograph is from a later era but shows Pumper no. 1 drafting from a cistern. Station no. 1 (1871–1938) can be seen to the right of the steamer's smokestack. *The Indianapolis Firefighters Museum.*

two were kept busy refilling the cisterns with water from nearby wells. Undoubtedly, this fire gave an extra push toward establishing a municipal water system in Indianapolis.

The fire was thought to have originated in the second-floor ticket office. However, the man who was selling tickets said everything appeared normal when he left the office to attend the lecture. The cause of the fire was believed to have been a small wood-burning heating stove in the ticket office that may have overheated.

The audience had evacuated safely, and flames were showing from a middle window on the second floor when the first fire apparatus arrived. Firefighters quickly extinguished this visible fire, and spectators thought it was all out. But unseen by them, flames were spreading toward the rear of the building on the second floor. From here, they burst out of a rear window and then quickly spread to the upper floors.

Within a short time, the auditorium and its balcony became fully involved. Shortly after this, the fire spread throughout the entire building. It had vented through the roof, and a large portion of the building's roof and the balcony collapsed into the third floor. By now, firefighters had written off the Morrison Opera House and were concentrating on keeping the fire from nearby structures. Part of the opera house's south wall collapsed into Maryland Street. The buildings on the south side of Maryland Street soon began to get very hot from radiant heat. Some of their wooden window frames were smoking by the time firefighters turned hose streams onto these buildings to cool them.

Despite the best efforts of the firefighters, the building to the north of the Morrison building was soon burning. That was the three-story brick Mothershead building. It was roughly 60 by 180 feet and occupied by J.W. Copeland and Company, a wholesale millinery company, and West, Morris and Gorrell, wholesale dealers of china and glass products. The third story was home to the National Business College. Again, firefighters fought tremendously and finally stopped the fire within this building around midnight. Despite this, the blaze destroyed the structure and its contents.

By 1:00 a.m. on January 18, the bright, leaping flames, which had attracted hundreds of spectators despite the cold temperatures, were mostly gone. Nothing remained of the Morrison Opera House or the Mothershead building except for smoking piles of debris and a few tottering brick walls.

The only injury was to a spectator named William Stevenson. He was deaf and couldn't hear the gong of a fire department hose reel as it arrived on the scene. As a result, he was run over and suffered a broken leg.

The monetary loss for the two buildings and their contents was almost $250,000 ($5,687,214). That loss included three hundred rifles owned by the national guard, along with their flags, uniforms and other equipment.

The remaining walls, some of which were dangerously unstable, were torn down within a few days after the fire. After contractors removed all the debris, construction began on new buildings to replace the two that were destroyed.

The new Morrison Opera House opened in October 1870. Despite retaining the "Opera House" name, this new four-story building had no auditorium or stage. Instead, it was constructed to house retail stores and offices. This second building, now called the Morrison Opera Place, still stands proudly.

In the 1950s, the building suffered the indignity of having its entire façade, including the windows on all its floors above the first, covered with ugly metal siding. Thankfully, this siding was removed in 1979, and the building's classic appearance was restored. It now looks much the same as it did when it was new in October 1870.

So, while the Morrison Opera House fire was large and destructive, no lives were lost. Today, most people have never heard of this fire. And that is almost entirely due to Reverend James Crawford. Without his calming efforts, we might be remembering a horrible tragedy in which many people died.

4

THE KENTUCKY AVENUE TRENCH COLLAPSE

Aside from roads and bridges, sewers are some of the earliest examples of infrastructure constructed within Indianapolis. And surprisingly, some of these sewers, built in the early 1870s, are still part of the vast network of sewers used in Indianapolis.

On the morning of Wednesday, September 20, 1871, crews were at work, digging a trench to install new sewers. They were working along Kentucky Avenue, a little south of Georgia Street. Today, Kentucky Avenue has been abandoned and built over, so it no longer exists within the Mile Square. The Indiana Convention Center now covers the area where this incident occurred.

Workers building the sewer used a method known as "cut and cover." First, they would dig a large trench, and then masons working at the bottom would lay a stone and brick base for the sewer floor. Next, they would build an archway of bricks, making an enclosure for the wastewater and stormwater flow. Finally, the workers would backfill the ditch with dirt to cover the completed sewer. Then they would start digging another trench where the first trench ended, starting a new section of the sewer at the end of the previously completed sewer. That was part of an extensive civic project building sewers throughout downtown Indianapolis.

The trench being dug was twelve feet wide and twenty-two feet deep. This portion of it was a few hundred feet in length. Remember, this was built in 1871, and there was no mechanized equipment to dig the trench. Instead, it was dug by men using nothing but hand tools. Workers then drove in vertical planks on both sides of the trench to prevent the sides from caving in. These boards were cross braced against each other using horizontal planks.

Work was proceeding when, around 8:30 a.m., a portion of the trench, thirty feet in length, collapsed. The collapse came without warning. It was later speculated that vibrations from the movement of trains on a track about seventy feet away might have been the cause of the collapse.

Whatever the reason, both sides of the trench collapsed. The planks that were used for shoring up the sides fell toward each other, meeting in the middle. These boards' upside-down V configuration made a protected void at the bottom of the excavation. It was hoped that the men in the collapsed trench would be found alive and protected within this space. Fortunately, two men, John Fox and another man who was not identified, were working near the top of the excavation. They managed to scramble from the trench as it collapsed. Both men were slightly injured but survived. The other men were at the bottom of the excavation and had no chance of escaping. It was initially thought that nine men were at work at the bottom of the trench.

The crew foreman, Jesse Whitsit, and John Miller, another crew member who'd formerly been a miner, began efforts to rescue the trapped men. They managed to make their way through the dirt and broken planks into the protected space. Unfortunately, Henry Barnes, the first person they found, had not survived. It was believed that he'd suffered a broken neck, possibly from being struck by the planking as the sides fell in. Struggling to dig through the dirt and splintered boards, they could hear the voices of three other trapped men. However, they were able to free only one of them. Rescuers brought Tim Lyons to the surface, injured but still alive. The other two men couldn't be rescued then. However, they assured their would-be rescuers they were safe. They also thought they had enough air to survive until they could be freed.

Word quickly spread about the trapped men. Soon, more than fifty men were at work, desperately digging to free those who were still trapped. Meanwhile, a large crowd, estimated at several thousand, had gathered in the area. Some were the wives and family members of the laborers employed at the site. They were frantic with grief, trying to find out if their husbands or loved ones were among those trapped.

Chief of Police Eli Thompson and a squad of his men hurried to the scene to maintain control. The police used ropes as makeshift barriers to keep the crowd back. That also helped lessen the potential of vibrations from the crowd's feet, causing a further collapse.

A lengthy delay ensued when it was discovered that the sides of the trench were in danger of further collapse. As a result, the men who were digging for the victims were forced to turn their attention to moving dirt away from the sides of the excavation. In addition, more planking was brought in to reinforce the sides of the trench. Only after doing all this could they resume the search for victims.

By now, enough time had elapsed that the rescuers and everyone in the crowd had given up all hope of finding anyone alive. Thus, they were surprised when someone was heard groaning in the trench. Nevertheless, they quickly renewed their digging efforts. The man, later identified as John Gibson, was finally rescued at about 2:00 p.m. (That was over five hours after the collapse.) After being given brandy as a stimulant, Gibson told his rescuers he was having no trouble breathing. However, he said his legs, which had been pinned under some timbers, were hurting. He also told the authorities that he had heard other men's voices close by him, but they'd eventually grown silent and he feared they'd died.

When rescuers finally reached the rest of the trapped men, what they found was even worse than feared. Instead of the nine men who were thought to have been working in the trench when it collapsed, there'd actually been twelve. Only the two men who had managed to get out as the collapse occurred and the two who were rescued had survived. Eight bodies were found at the bottom of the trench. Even the two men who'd talked to rescuers and told them they thought they had enough air to survive had died. Coroner James Hedges thought all the victims had died of asphyxiation—except the man with a broken neck. The last body was not recovered until late that evening.

The men who died were all working in what we would call a "minimum wage job." A few were married. All of them were immigrants, six from Ireland and two from England. One had just come to America a few weeks before the accident. He'd left his wife behind in England and was working to earn enough money to pay her fare so she could join him in this country.

Several concerts and benefits were held for the victims' families in the next few weeks. Sadly, most of their surviving family members did not have much in the way of insurance or other assets.

The *Indianapolis Evening Journal* of September 20, 1871, described one humorous incident on an otherwise sad day. The paper said that a "lusty Irish woman" had learned of the collapse. She'd been shopping and had her market basket with her as she hurried to the scene, knowing her husband was working on the sewer project. As she arrived and saw the extent of the incident, the paper said she "let go of her basket, toppled over backward, and shrieked: 'Pat! Oh my God, Pat!'" Luckily, her husband was not trapped, and he was quickly by her side, reassuring her that he was alright. As she heard his voice, she loudly exclaimed, "Damn your eyes, Pat! I thought you were in there!"

Funeral services for six of the victims, who were of Catholic faith, were held on Thursday at 3:00 p.m. These six deceased were Jerry Sullivan, John Carr, Thomas Kennedy, Henry Dugan, John Haley and John Greeley. The services were held at St. John the Evangelist Catholic Church. This church was newly built in 1871 and is still in use, located on the east side of Capitol Avenue between Maryland and Georgia Streets. The September 24, 1871 edition of the *Indianapolis People* newspaper reported that the funeral procession consisted of 6 hearses and 140 carriages. It also said that an "immense number" of citizens attended.

Protestant services for the two other victims, Jesse Brookstone and Henry Barnes, were held on Friday morning. These men were natives of England and had only recently immigrated to America. They had no known relatives in this country. The September 23, 1871 edition of the *Indianapolis Evening Journal* reported, "The services were well attended and very impressively conducted, and although the poor men were almost total strangers in our city, every possible respect and attention was paid to their remains."

James H. Hedges, the Marion County coroner, empaneled a jury to hold an inquest. The contractors testified that they'd used this same "cut and cover" process to build sewers elsewhere in downtown Indianapolis with no problems. They told of the standard precautions they took when excavating and that they'd used extra caution due to the proximity of the train tracks. Nevertheless, the contractors felt that the loose nature of the soil in this particular area, combined with the vibration from the trains passing nearby, caused the collapse. After hearing testimony from thirty-five witnesses, the six men of the jury ruled that the trench collapse had been an unavoidable accident. They further ruled that the contractors and any other persons were fully exonerated from any blame for the incident.

The Monday, September 25, 1871 edition of the *Indianapolis News* noted, "Work on the Kentucky Avenue sewer was resumed this morning." However, problems continued to plague the project. On October 13, 1871, the same newspaper reported, "The East Street sewer caved in last night, but no one happened to be in the excavation."

5

THE 1882 FLOOD

Pogue's Run is a small stream that begins on the east side of Indianapolis and winds its way toward the southwest, eventually emptying into the White River. On its relatively short journey, it passes through the southeast corner of the Mile Square downtown area. When Alexander Ralston laid out Indianapolis, he had to work around what would later become known as Pogue's Run. That is obvious when you look at his original plan for the city. The neat and orderly gridwork of streets, which is very evident in the other three quadrants of his plan, is spoiled by the meandering course of this stream as it makes its way across the southeastern quadrant.

These days, Pogue's Run still follows much the same course it always has. However, most people are unaware that it still flows through the downtown area. This is due to an ambitious engineering project that was started in 1914 to allow the waters of Pogue's Run to run through a series of concrete tunnels, hiding them from view beneath most of the urban streetscapes.

The stream is named in honor of George Pogue, an early resident of central Indiana. In the spring of 1821, some of Mr. Pogue's horses were stolen. He blamed Natives who, at that time, still lived in the area. One morning later that same spring, Pogue left his home to look for the horses and never returned. A few weeks later, one of Pogue's sons saw a Native man wearing what he believed was some of his father's clothing. A group of Pogue's friends subsequently searched several Native camps in the area, but neither George Pogue nor his remains were ever found. After more than two hundred years, the missing man remains Indianapolis's oldest cold case.

Due mainly to claims made by Mr. Pogue and his family, who said they'd been the first non-Natives to settle in the area, the stream was christened in his honor. However, there were disagreements over who the actual "first settler" was, since John McCormick and his family also claimed this distinction. Historians have long disputed whether Pogue or McCormick deserved the accolade. But all arguments aside, the watercourse received Pogue's name.

The stream had long been a problem for residents of Indianapolis. It often flooded after heavy showers. And in warm weather, the slow-moving waters were breeding grounds for mosquitos. These insects were, at best, a nuisance, and at their worst, they spread disease. In addition, the ground around the stream was swampy and unsuitable for building homes or other structures.

As mentioned, Pogue's Run was sometimes prone to flooding and had done so several times in the past. The last major flood before this occurred in September 1866. It caused extensive property damage and, sadly, the deaths of three people.

The flood of 1882 began rather quietly. The rain started around midnight on Saturday, June 10. At first, it was merely an inconvenience. Some outdoor events that were originally scheduled for Saturday or Sunday afternoons were postponed or canceled. Worshipers headed for church on Sunday morning needed their umbrellas. The rain continued intermittently for the next couple of days, coming down just enough to be a nuisance. Then on the evening of Tuesday, June 13, it began to storm, and overnight, the rain grew much more intense. By Wednesday morning, the streets were flooding, and their gutters overflowed. Usually tranquil waterways, such as Pleasant Run and Pogue's Run, spilled from their banks.

According to the June 14, 1882 *Indianapolis News*, several trees were toppled by high winds. Lightning was also a problem. A home at 578 Park Avenue was struck and received $100 ($2,922) in damages. Another residence at 625 East Ohio Street suffered damage to its chimney and roof from a lightning strike. James T. Layman, the president of the board of aldermen for the City of Indianapolis, reported seeing a small tornado, but no one else confirmed his sighting.

The *Indianapolis Journal* of June 15, 1882, reported that, according to the U.S. Weather Bureau, 3.51 inches of rain fell between midnight on June 10 and 7:00 a.m. on June 15. The majority of this rain fell overnight on June 13 and 14. According to the June 17, 1882 *Indianapolis Leader*, Judge Franklin, an old resident who said he'd lived in the area since "the best part of our city was a forest," declared that the rain was the heaviest he had ever witnessed.

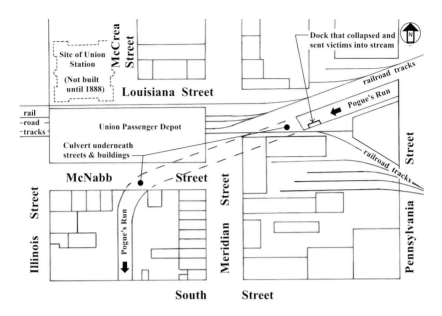

A map showing the path Pogue's Run took near the Union Passenger Depot. The dock that collapsed and sent ten people to their deaths is noted. *Map by author.*

As mentioned, the strong winds brought down numerous trees throughout the area, while the water swept away wooden fences, sheds, small barns and other outbuildings. And in this era, before indoor plumbing was common, outdoor privies also fell victim to the onslaught of the floodwaters. All this debris piled up at various locations, causing makeshift dams in the waterways, which caused additional flooding in these areas.

But unfortunately, aside from all the property damage the flood caused, it was also responsible for the deaths of several people. These deaths occurred near Union Station. However, that was not the historic railroad station still standing today. That structure wasn't built until 1888. Instead, it was the original Union Passenger Depot constructed in 1853. That first station was located between Meridian and Illinois Streets on the south side of Louisiana Street. That is now the site of the present Union Station's train shed. However, that structure is larger, extending another block west to Capitol Avenue. Another change is that the railroad tracks are elevated today to minimize their interference with pedestrian and vehicle traffic. In 1882, all the railroad tracks were at street level.

After passing beneath Pennsylvania Street, Pogue's Run ran in the open until about eighty feet east of Meridian Street. Pogue's Run then disappeared into a concrete culvert, six to eight feet in diameter and about three hundred feet long. Next, it passed underneath railroad tracks, part of a warehouse, Meridian Street, the southeastern corner of the Union Depot and McNabb Street while turning south. Pogue's Run then reappeared for about two hundred feet before disappearing into another culvert beneath South Street. A wooden dock was constructed on the stream's south side, between Pennsylvania and Meridian Streets.

About thirty to forty men, women and some children were on this dock, watching the churning, turbulent water as it flowed past them. Just before 9:00 a.m., Daniel Whitcomb, the superintendent of the Union Railway Company, saw the crowd on the dock. He shouted a warning, saying he didn't think the structure would safely hold the number of people on it. A few left, but most in the crowd ignored his warning. Shortly after this, William Jackson, an official with the Union Depot, also cautioned spectators, telling them the dock looked unstable. Despite these warnings, the small dock remained crowded with people who were laughing and talking, seemingly unaware of any possible danger.

Suddenly, at about 9:20 a.m., the dock collapsed, sending the crowd of about thirty spectators plunging into the rushing water. Other people who were standing nearby quickly sprang into action. Cyrus Bartlett was off work due to the flood. He'd been standing nearby and promptly dove into the water, rescuing two young women. Other rescuers rushed to the mouth of the culvert. Using ropes and anything else they could find, they plucked victims from the water before they could be swept into the culvert. About fifteen victims were rescued in this manner. The rushing water propelled the remaining victims through the culvert beneath the streets and buildings. The next stretch of open water was south of the depot, between McNabb and South Streets, where more rescues occurred. Fortunately, all of the children who fell in were rescued.

Two teenagers and five adults who drowned after the structure fell were not as lucky. The teenage victims were Edward Tilford and Katie Gilderman, the only female victim. The adult victims were Abraham Saunders, George Smith, John Scoville, James McMinnis and Patrick Gaven. The remains of these seven victims were recovered over the next several hours.

Annie Sensenbrenner, Florence Lynn and Katie Gilderman had all been employed at the Barnett and Elliot Wholesale Shoe Company, located on South Meridian Street. They were about sixteen years old and off work because of the flood. Annie and Florence were both rescued, but Katie could not be saved. Edward Tilford, the other teenage victim, was also sixteen. He'd worked at Augustus Kiefer's wholesale drug company. These young people were employed full time, earning money to help their families. They had all been standing on the dock when it fell.

In addition to these seven victims, three other men who were known to have been on the dock were missing and presumed dead. Their fates were confirmed when their bodies were located over the next few days. All three had passed through Pogue's Run and on into the White River. On Wednesday, Patrick O'Brien's body was found tangled among some driftwood near the Belt Railroad bridge over the river. The body of Charles G. Herman was found on Friday, close to where Pleasant Run empties into the White River. Thomas Daily's body was the last to be located. It was recovered early Saturday evening, about three-fourths of a mile south of Maywood, near Indianapolis. It was found by Daily's brother, who, for several days, had been searching the White River for his brother's body.

Although this was the last victim reported missing from Indianapolis, there were reports from Waverly, Morgan County, of two more bodies found there, floating in the White River. Where these bodies may have come from was never established.

A total of ten people died in Pogue's Run. That was Indianapolis's greatest loss of life since the state fair steam engine explosion in 1869. The Marion County coroner, Dr. Allison Maxwell, held an inquest a few days later. His findings were as follows: "The deceased all came to their deaths by accidental drowning, by being precipitated into Pogue's Run, just above the Union Depot. I fail to find that anyone is especially responsible for the accident, and I attribute the disaster to the large number of persons who were standing on the platform and caused it to break. I also find that the deceased were all warned of the danger."

After the floodwaters had subsided the next day, firefighters waded through the culvert underneath Meridian and McNabb Streets and the Union Depot. That was the culvert through which the waters of Pogue's Run flowed. The firefighters searched the dark tunnel using lanterns to ensure no bodies had been snagged by obstructions. Luckily, none were found.

Not all victims who fell from the dock were sorry about their ordeal. One of them, Henry Sendo, actually seemed happy to have undergone his accidental dunking. Mr. Sendo explained in the June 17, 1882 *Indianapolis News* that he had "been lame for years with rheumatism and at times unable to walk." However, he claimed to have been cured of this problem after falling into Pogue's Run.

The flooding hit particularly hard in the downtown area. Pogue's Run reached its high point between 8:00 and 9:00 a.m. on Wednesday. Then water began flowing through the streets and reached depths of three feet on some downtown streets. Basements in several downtown buildings soon began flooding.

Workers at the Johnston and Erwin Wholesale Dry Goods Company had a close call. The company, located at 211 South Meridian Street, had a basement full of merchandise. Aware that nearby basements were flooding, the workers scrambled to move everything from their basement to the upper floors. Suddenly, the basement wall of the adjoining building broke, and water began pouring into Johnston and Erwin's basement. The G.W. Stout building next door had already flooded, and that water had weakened Johnston and Erwin's basement walls. The sudden influx of water quickly flooded the basement, and the workers had to swim for their lives. According to the June 15, 1882 *Indianapolis Journal*, Daniel Erwin, one of the owners, was in the basement overseeing the work. He and the other men jumped into an elevator when the wall broke. Unfortunately, the inrushing water quickly filled the basement before the elevator even reached the first floor. Luckily, everyone made it out safely.

Dozens of downtown buildings had their basements flooded, many losing valuable merchandise stored there. In addition, some buildings had damage done to their basement walls and foundations by the floodwater. The *Indianapolis Journal* estimated losses downtown at over $60,000 ($1,753,000). And this figure was for only the merchandise lost. No estimate for damage to the buildings was given.

There were reports of several close calls. For example, the June 14, 1882 edition of the *Indianapolis News* reported that Nellie Lusher, whose age was not given but whom the paper called a "young girl," fell into some water near the area of English Avenue and Cedar Street. Ellsbury H. Perkins, who also happened to work for the *News*, rescued her.

This same newspaper also reported the rescue of two boys after they fell into the State Ditch while floating on pieces of wood in the swollen stream. They were pulled out "with difficulty" by a man as the small waterway crossed underneath College Avenue on the north side of Indianapolis. Neither of the boys nor their rescuer was identified in the article.

J.W. LaPorte and his family lived at 311 East Washington Street. Like so many others, their basement had become inundated with rain. On Thursday, June 15, Laporte's four-year-old daughter somehow fell into the flooded basement. Young Edna couldn't swim but, luckily, was rescued by a family member. She survived but was very ill for a time due to swallowing some of the dirty water.

Some people still managed to find fun amid all the chaos. John Roland, who lived on East Ohio Street, was somewhat surprised when he woke up Wednesday morning and heard laughing and giggling coming from his kitchen. Being the father of two young boys, this was not unusual; however, what got his attention was the splashing he also heard. Upon investigating, he was amazed to find his sons swimming in the kitchen. Unknown to him, the floodwaters had entered the back of his home, where the kitchen was, and filled it deep enough to give his sons a place to swim and frolic.

The rushing water swept away several street bridges. Some were wooden, while others were built of steel. Railroad bridges were also affected, with several being swept away by the rushing water. In at least one case, railroad officials took the extreme measure of parking heavy freight cars on a bridge, attempting to add weight and hold it in place. It was successful, as the bridge stayed where it was needed.

Leander A. Fulmer, the city's street commissioner, reported on the losses that Indianapolis bridges had sustained. In the June 16, 1882 *Indianapolis News*, he said several bridges over Pogue's Run had been completely swept away. These included bridges at Brookside Avenue, Archer Street, Dorman Street and Park Avenue. The Archer Street bridge was built of iron and was carried intact downstream for more than a block. It then became lodged against another bridge on Michigan Street. Mr. Fulmer thought this bridge could be disassembled and then rebuilt in its original location. The other three bridges were destroyed and needed replacing. Other bridges suffered varying amounts of damage from flooding in Pogue's Run and needed repairs. They included the Market, New Jersey and Delaware Street bridges. Pleasant Run also flooded and damaged bridges at Reed and Shelby Streets. They were also repairable.

Amazingly, the floodwater was almost gone by the following evening, Thursday, June 15. Left in its wake were muddy streets and a lot of basements filled with dirty water. The fire department spent the next several days pumping out the basements of businesses and private residences all over the city.

However, Mother Nature was not finished with Indianapolis quite yet. Another strong storm hit the city on the evening of Friday, June 16, 1882. The weather had been clear, with temperatures in the nineties until about 4:00 p.m., when storm clouds started gathering. The wind began blowing strongly as the rain started again. Soon, thunder and lightning made another appearance, followed by hail. Once more, streets flooded and gutters overflowed. Numerous trees were blown down in the area, while many reported widows broken by hail or tree limbs. The June 17, 1882 *Indianapolis Journal* told of one large, old elm tree at Washington and Davidson Streets, which had been uprooted. It brought down several telegraph lines and damaged nearby homes as it fell. An apartment building in the 1900 block of North College Avenue lost its roof to high winds, as did a home near Broadway and Arch Streets.

The newspaper also mentioned that many trees across the area had been struck by lightning. The Indianapolis Fire Department was kept busy due to the many lightning strikes. A stable belonging to the George Sutter and Sons Ice Company burned down after being struck. It was located on the canal's east bank, just west of the present-day address of 1900 North Dr. M.L. King Jr. Street. That loss was estimated at $1,500 ($43,825). Another fire, caused by lightning, damaged the Woodburn "Sarven Wheel" Company at 430 South Illinois Street, with that loss set at $500 ($14,608).

Another problem for the fire department was its telegraphic alarm system. Because trees fell on some of its lines and the wind blew other wires together, causing short circuits, there were numerous problems with receiving and transmitting alarms. And Fire Station no. 6 at 533 West Washington Street suffered damage to its roof when the wind blew over the station's flagpole.

Sadly, this storm also caused a loss of life. As the storm began, Mrs. Jane Wallace, age sixty-six, went outside to close her basement's exterior door. The basement of her home at 29 Hosbrook Street already had five feet of water from the storm on Wednesday. She was attempting to close the door when she fell into the flooded basement. Due to her physical disabilities, she couldn't save herself and drowned.

On June 17, 1882, the *Indianapolis Leader* estimated that the total damages from both storms would easily exceed $200,000 ($5,843,333). The paper also noted that no one in Indianapolis had flood insurance.

In 1914, efforts were started to move the troublesome stream entirely underground in the downtown area. A few sections of Pogue's Run had already been diverted into concrete tunnels, like where the drownings occurred near Union Depot. The project cost $907,000 ($25,287,342) and took until late 1916 to finish. From about 1000 East Michigan Street to where it emptied into the White River, the waterway was now underground, directed into a series of concrete tunnels. The project was important for several reasons. It helped alleviate flooding and eliminated the noxious odors that sometimes came from the stream. But most significantly, routing the stream underground opened new areas of the city for development.

Today, thousands of people live, work, shop and even park their cars over Pogue's Run, without realizing that it still flows beneath them in concrete tunnels, on its way to empty into the White River.

6

THE BROAD RIPPLE BRIDGE COLLAPSE

Everything seemed routine as the train traveled south toward Indianapolis. The date was January 31, 1884. They were on time with no problems. Things were going so smoothly that John Brewer, the train's engineer, left his engine's cab and went back to ride in the baggage car before leaving the Carmel station. He told James Noonan, the train's fireman, to drive the train to its next stop in Broad Ripple. They'd left Carmel at 9:41 a.m. Following the Broad Ripple stop, they were due at the Indianapolis Union Station at 10:30 a.m.

The trip from Carmel to Broad Ripple was only a few miles, and the engineer had complete confidence in his fireman, knowing he could competently handle the train. After a few minutes of travel, they were about half a mile north of Broad Ripple, approaching the bridge over White River. As the locomotive began the crossing, the fireman, Noonan, felt the bridge sinking—an obvious sign of danger. Instinctively, he pulled the throttle wide open, hoping to get the train across the bridge before anything could happen. But it was too late. The locomotive and its tender made it safely across. Unfortunately, the rest of the train plunged through a break in the bridge. It fell about twenty feet into the river, which was eight to ten feet deep in that area. The bridge had broken just before the middle of the three abutments holding the bridge above the river.

Besides the steam locomotive and its tender, the train had only three other cars: a baggage car and two passenger cars. The baggage car fell through first. Then the first passenger car fell directly on top of the baggage car, crushing both badly. The second passenger car wound up at an angle, with its front end in the water and its rear dangling on the edge of the bridge. Coal-burning stoves heated all three cars. These stoves fell over, and their hot coals spilled out, quickly starting fires in the wreckage. Three men died in the ruins of the baggage car, and two more perished in the first passenger car. The sixth victim was working on the bridge at the time of the accident.

James Noonan, the fireman who was running the train at the time of the collapse, quickly stopped the locomotive and got off to check what had happened. He knew that his locomotive was still on the tracks and seemed alright. Looking behind him, he found that the tender had derailed but was on solid ground. However, the rest of the train had disappeared from view. Ominously, he could see the broken bridge and a thin curl of smoke rising beneath that. Running to the bridge, he was horrified to see two cars lying in a shattered heap down in the river. The third car was tilted at a precarious angle. The broken tracks barely held up its rear on the north side of the bridge. The front part of the car had fallen through the bridge and was down in the water. Pieces of the bridge were scattered among the train's wreckage, and smoke was beginning to come from the ruins. Noonan could hear cries for help but could not immediately do anything. He had no easy way to get down the steep bank to the river. And even if he could, he would then need a boat to get out to where the wreckage was. Knowing his only choice was to get help, he returned to the locomotive. He quickly drove it toward the station in Broad Ripple, which was only about half a mile away. He frantically blew the whistle on the short trip, letting everyone in the town know something was drastically wrong.

Residents of Broad Ripple, startled by the train's insistent whistle, hurried to the station to see what the problem was. When they learned of the bridge collapse, they rushed to the wreck site to render whatever aid they could give the survivors. At the same time, people who lived near the ill-fated bridge heard the noise as the cars crashed into the river. Knowing that what they heard must mean trouble, they hastened toward the noise and discovered the awful scene. Luckily, some had boats nearby and rowed out to the wreck site. Unable to get too close due to the heat from the burning cars, they were still able to rescue survivors. Others had buckets, and while standing on the small islands where the bridge abutments were, they tried throwing water on the fire. These efforts were done mostly in vain because the fire was just too intense. It overwhelmed the small amount of water they could throw. All three cars were fully engulfed in flames in a short time. The small bucket brigade focused on the wooden bridge, which was also in danger of catching fire from the burning train cars. They were successful in this endeavor.

The people of Broad Ripple brought the survivors back to their town, where they were placed in the care of local physician Dr. Joseph Bates. The train's conductor, William Losey, sent a telegram to the Louisville, New Albany and Chicago Railroad officials at Union Station in Indianapolis. The telegram informed the officials of the railroad, commonly known as "the Monon," that there'd been a wreck and that most of the train had plunged into the river.

Upon receiving the telegram, railroad officials assembled a relief train to head to the wreck site. They put together a crew of workers with a variety of tools. They also sent messages to several doctors, asking them to hurry to the station to board the train. They collected medical supplies from a drugstore near the station. And they also got workers and caskets from Kregelo and Whitsett, Funeral Directors. They wanted to be prepared for whatever they might find.

The relief train was delayed but finally reached Broad Ripple at 11:30 a.m., about an hour and a half after the wreck. Five doctors were on board: Joseph Eastman, William Wands, Henry Jameson, William Stocker and Allison Maxwell. Conveniently, Dr. Maxwell also served as the Marion County coroner. When the train arrived in Broad Ripple, it stopped briefly, and two doctors got off to assist Dr. Bates, who was treating the survivors at his house. The train, with the other doctors, continued to the wreck site.

At the scene, they found that the survivors had all been rescued. There was nothing left to do but recover the bodies. The fire had consumed all the wooden parts of the train. Spectators described how, as the portion of the wooden train cars above the water burned, they became lighter and floated higher in the water. This newly exposed wood then caught fire. In this manner, all the wood burned away, leaving nothing but the metal parts of the train. Unfortunately, this meant that the victims' bodies were severely burned.

As was usual in that era, the newspapers were very graphic in their descriptions of the unfortunate casualties. For example, the *Indianapolis Journal* of February 1, 1884, told of one body that was "charred and shapeless, unrecognizable as the frame of a human being." Another was said to be "only the trunk of a body, with one leg remaining."

The same paper also described the grief of one witness as a body was recovered. Someone in the recovery crew shouted to the crowd watching on the shore, "This is probably the body of John Bray!" Then, suddenly, a pitiful shriek was heard as one of the spectators screamed, "My God, it's my father!" He hadn't known his father was on the train. The younger man happened to be nearby when he heard about the wreck and went to the scene. The Bray family lived in Deming, about twenty miles away. Bray's body was placed in a wagon to be taken away. His son draped himself over the wagon, grieving wildly, exclaiming, "My God, this is horrible! It is too much!" He was finally led away from the body, which the paper said was a "ghastly and sickening sight."

The *Indianapolis Journal*'s article also described the morbid curiosity of some citizens in Broad Ripple, particularly that of the women. It told of how the burned bodies lay in open wooden coffins, covered by only white muslin cloth. As these coffins were waiting to be taken by train to Indianapolis, they were lying on the station's platform. Many people were trying to look at the coffins' contents, and no one attempted to stop them. But oddly, the paper noted, "The greatest curiosity seemed to be manifested by the women, a dozen or more of whom could be seen standing on the platform. They were not at all backward in removing the temporary covering from the bodies and displaying them to the gaze of the newcomers. Some of these women were accompanied by their children."

As was another custom of that era, the remains were placed on public display at Kregelo and Whitsett, Funeral Directors. The *Indianapolis Journal* of February 1, 1884, estimated that "they were viewed by probably a thousand people during the evening and night."

All the bodies were recovered that same day—except for the body of Thomas Parrs. Mr. Parr was the superintendent of a crew of men working on the bridge at the time of the accident. His body was known to still be in the river, probably trapped beneath the wreckage. There were also reports that there could be bodies of other passengers trapped under this wreckage, although no one was reported missing. Three undertakers used poles with hooks to search the water around the wreckage for bodies, but none were found. All the men working on the bridge were accounted for except for Thomas Parr.

As can be imagined, survivors described the scenes inside both passenger cars as chaotic. W.A. Seamans, who owned the Westfield Mill and had formerly been the sheriff of Hamilton County, was riding in the first passenger car. He said that he'd been seated in the rear of the car. Suddenly, he heard a crash and felt the car falling. He tried to stand but was pinned to the floor by debris. Then somehow, he escaped the wreckage; though later, he couldn't remember how he had done so. As he fled the wrecked car, he heard the cries of other injured people. However, due to his injuries, he could do nothing to help them. He was suffering from a broken right arm, cuts on his head and severe pain in his side.

Lynn Clark, originally from Westfield, Indiana, but now living in Kansas, made a dramatic escape. He'd been visiting relatives in the area and was going to Indianapolis to take a train back home. After the accident, he found himself covered in debris, with a heavy wood beam pinning one of his legs. The January 31, 1884 edition of the *Indianapolis News* described the struggle to save Mr. Clark. Two passengers, Dr. C.C. Loder and J.B. Horton, said they tried to assist Clark. However, they could find nothing to cut or move the heavy beam. As the flames moved closer, Clark begged them, "For God's sake, don't desert me!" "We did not desert him," said Dr. Loder, "until the flames scorched us, and we almost suffocated with smoke." Before Dr. Loder was forced to abandon Clark, he broke a nearby window. Miraculously, minutes later, the fire burned the beam enough that Clark could finally free himself. He then crawled to safety through the window that Dr. Loder had broken. Lynn Clark suffered burns and internal injuries. Newspapers gave his condition as critical and said he was not likely to survive. However, this author could find no report that, in the following months, he'd died from his injuries.

At least a dozen men and women and one small child were in the rear passenger car. Luckily, none were seriously injured. Joseph Claybaugh from Frankfort, Indiana, was seated in the middle of the car. In the February 1, 1884 *Indianapolis Journal*, he said he was "thrown over the seat in front of him by the sudden and violent plunging against the forward cars." He praised his fellow passengers, saying, "There was no screaming, and the other passengers, although realizing that the train had been wrecked, did not become unreasonably excited." Since their car was relatively undamaged, they didn't realize the full extent of the wreck until they got out.

They could make their way out of the car, even though it was tilted at an extreme angle. They managed to climb across the seats to the rear platform. From there, they climbed up the broken bridge using the ties of the track like a ladder. Then they carefully walked across the bridge to the north shore.

With the dead and injured victims taken care of, attention could now be focused on why the bridge suffered a partial collapse. It was only about seventeen months old, having been constructed in September 1882. Since then, there had been several trains that passed over it daily. In fact, only about an hour before the accident, another train had used the bridge. That train had a larger steam engine and fourteen fully loaded freight cars, making it much heavier than the passenger train. Yet it crossed this same bridge with no problem.

One major clue was that the bridge was being worked on at the time of the accident. It's unclear why this bridge, which was less than two years old, needed work. Presumably, it was just routine maintenance, although some reports indicate that the bridge was being reinforced. The crew consisted of the foreman, Thomas Parr, with Ben White, Charles Parker and George Beyer. Parr had experience building and repairing bridges, while the other men were laborers working under his direction. All four men, along with part of the bridge and the train cars, fell into the river. The wreckage did not trap Parker and Beyer, and they were uninjured. White was injured but freed himself from under the wreckage. Thomas Parr was trapped beneath the debris and drowned. His body was recovered two days later. About 130 feet of the bridge collapsed into the river between the northern and middle abutments.

The *Indianapolis Journal* of February 1, 1884, mentioned that there had been rumors a few weeks previously that a train had broken through this same bridge near Broad Ripple. A quick investigation by the paper proved this to be false.

That coincidentally was the same day a similar accident happened in southern Indiana. On December 24, 1883, another Monon train broke through a bridge near Salem, Indiana. That accident took the lives of nine people.

Then two weeks before the accident near Broad Ripple took place, that same rumor was again spread and, once more, was found to be untrue. Unfortunately, it was never learned who was spreading these rumors.

Because of the type of bridge involved in the accident, railroad companies across the United States were very interested in learning what caused this collapse. The bridge type was known as the Howe truss bridge. In the February 2, 1884 edition of the *Indianapolis Journal*, a man, who was unnamed in the article but described as "one of the best Chief Engineers," said that at least 60 percent of the railroad bridges in this country were built using this design. Furthermore, he said the design was considered "the safest and surest bridges constructed." He also claimed that "a Howe truss bridge made of straw would hold a train."

Dr. Allison Maxwell, the Marion County coroner, began an inquest into the accident on February 1, 1884. Over the next eleven days, he interviewed many people about the accident. These included train crew members, bridge builders, the men who had been repairing the bridge at the time of the accident, passengers, railroad officials and anyone who could shed light on what had gone wrong.

The fact that the train's engineer left the fireman in charge and wasn't even in the train's cab at the time of the accident didn't seem to be a factor. It was mentioned only briefly during the inquest, according to newspaper reports. Instead, the main focus seemed to be the work that was being done to the bridge at the time of the collapse.

On February 12, 1884, Coroner Maxwell announced his verdict. He ruled that the collapse was caused by the breaking of iron rods that were used to brace the bridge. "Temporary rods" were in place while "permanent rods" were loosened to strengthen the bridge. So, who was responsible? According to the February 13, 1884 *Indianapolis News*, "The question of responsibility is left open."

James Roosevelt, the president of the Louisville, New Albany and Chicago Railroad, also known as the Monon, visited the accident site a few days later. He expressed his regret over the deaths and injuries and thanked those who helped in the rescue and recovery operations. James was the father of future United States president Franklin D. Roosevelt, who'd turned two years old the day before the accident.

Today, there is still a bridge over the White River at about the same location as the ill-fated bridge. But now, that bridge is part of a walking trail that follows the route of the former rail line into Indianapolis. It honors the long-gone railroad with its name: the Monon Walking Trail. An estimated four thousand people use the trail every day. However, very few of them are aware of the deaths of six people that occurred when the predecessor of this bridge broke.

7

THE BOWEN-MERRILL FIRE

The worst loss of life ever suffered by members of the Indianapolis Fire Department occurred on March 17, 1890, during a fire at the Bowen-Merrill Bookstore. For many years, the death toll was thought to have been thirteen. But in truth, there were additional victims whom history had largely forgotten.

Now, research done by the staff of the Indianapolis Firefighters Museum has found three other victims whose deaths were also the result of the injuries they suffered in the fire and subsequent collapse. These victims all died in the early twentieth century. However, these deaths weren't listed as line of duty deaths at that time for unknown reasons. The death toll, now recognized by the Indianapolis Fire Department, is sixteen firefighters.

Bowen-Merrill's address was 16 and 18 West Washington Street. That was on the north side of Washington Street in the first quarter block west of Meridian Street.

Today, that location is home to the historic H.P. Wasson and Company building. The site of the tragic fire was the west end of the Wasson building. Wasson's western wall is where Bowen-Merrill's west wall once stood, while Bowen-Merrill's eastern wall would have been thirty-four feet (the width of the Bowen-Merrill building) east of that point. The Bowen-Merrill building was four stories tall, while Wasson's is eight stories tall. In 1999, a historical marker was placed near the site of the Bowen-Merrill building, memorializing the tragic event.

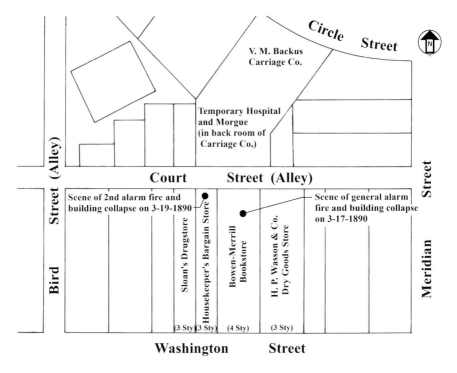

A map showing the area around Bowen-Merrill. Two days after the fire, the removal of the bookstore's façade caused structural damage to Wasson's and a fire and collapse in the Housekeeper's Bargain Store. *Map by author.*

The building had been home to a bookstore since sometime in the 1840s. The original store was named the C.B. Davis and Company Bookstore. Then through various investments and buyouts, that same bookstore became H.F. West and Company and then West and Stewart. It became Stewart and Bowen in 1855, when Silas Bowen became a partner. Five years later, he increased his investment, and the firm became Bowen, Stewart and Company. In 1885, Bowen, Stewart and Company merged with another local bookstore called Merrill, Meigs and Company. The book and stationery store, still at its original location, then became the Bowen-Merrill Company. Its specialty was publishing and selling law books, but it also sold books of all types for the general public. In addition, it sold stationery and other kinds of paper goods—even toilet paper.

Silas Bowen bought the original building at 18 West Washington Street in 1860. That building had been constructed in the early 1840s with brick walls on a stone foundation. Then in 1869, Mr. Bowen also purchased the building next door on the east side of the first building. This building's address was

16 West Washington Street. It was of similar construction and built at about the same time as the other building. After purchasing this second property, Mr. Bowen had both remodeled to be one structure. Workers removed each building's front brick walls and replaced them with a single cast-iron façade. They also removed the common brick wall between the two buildings, except for the part of that wall in the basement. Replacing the wall was a series of vertical iron columns. They were about eight inches in diameter and spaced evenly from the front to the rear of the building. The columns were placed on top of the wall in the basement. They extended from the floor to the ceiling of every floor and helped support each floor and the roof.

Two skylights were put in the roof with openings on each floor, providing natural light to every floor except the basement. There were also gaslights used for illumination throughout the building.

Mr. Bowen now had one building that was 34 by 120 feet. It was three stories tall for the first 50 feet back from the front wall and then two stories in height for the remaining 70 feet. In 1872, he added one story to each portion, making the building four stories tall in the front and three stories throughout the rest of the structure. At the same time, the three-story cast-iron façade was removed and replaced by a similar four-story façade. In 1886, Mr. Bowen added another story in the rear. The entire building was now four stories tall.

But it was still supported by its original foundation, a stone foundation designed for a two- and three-story building, a foundation that had never been updated or reinforced to compensate for the extra walls, extra floors and additional floor loads it now held.

MONDAY, MARCH 17

The disaster occurred on Monday, March 17, 1890—St. Patrick's Day. The temperature was cool. The *Indianapolis Journal* of March 18, 1890, reported that the low temperature for Monday had been 30 degrees Fahrenheit, while the high was 46 degrees Fahrenheit. The skies were cloudy.

A fire was discovered a little after 3:00 p.m. Somehow, paper goods near the front of the basement caught fire. Harvey Johnson, an employee, was in the basement and spotted the fire first. He fought the flames with a fire extinguisher, but it had little effect on the rapidly spreading fire. The store began filling with smoke, and employees and customers were forced to flee outside. Someone ran to the corner of Washington and Meridian

Streets and pulled alarm box no. 45. The alarm office dispatched the first companies at 3:08 p.m.

Hose no. 7, located on Maryland Street just east of Meridian Street, was on the scene quickly. James Davis, the Assistant Chief Fire Engineer, later credited the 7s with having water on the fire just three minutes after receiving the alarm. Soon, the entire first alarm assignment was working. Entry into the building was difficult due to the thick smoke. Firefighters directed hoses into the grates in the front sidewalk that they'd forced open. The store's basement extended beneath the sidewalk, so these grates opened directly into it.

Meanwhile, Engine no. 2's crew entered the basement from the rear of the building, where they encountered heavy fire and smoke. Chief Fire Engineer Frank Dougherty crawled through the front door and managed to get about fifteen feet inside the structure. Despite the thick smoke, he could see flames coming up through the floor on the west side of the building. Knowing this indicated the floor was already compromised, he ordered all companies to evacuate the building and begin an exterior attack.

Chief Dougherty requested a second alarm at 3:30 p.m. and a third alarm at 3:40 p.m., quickly followed by a general alarm at 3:41 p.m. That called every IFD apparatus to the scene. Despite all these companies, the fire was still spreading. It also attracted much attention, with thousands of spectators watching the firefighting.

There were concerns about the buildings on each side of Bowen-Merrill. On the west side was the Housekeeper's Bargain Store, located in the Becker building at 20 West Washington Street. That was a three-story brick building, 18 by 120 feet. The eastern exposure was the H.P. Wasson Dry Goods Store, whose address was 12 and 14 West Washington Street. That building measured 33 by 120 feet and was a three-story brick structure. Both stores suffered a lot of smoke damage, and after Bowen-Merrill collapsed, they also suffered significant structural damage. Other nearby businesses reported varying amounts of damage, all due to the heavy smoke from Bowen-Merrill.

Washington Street was broad enough that buildings across the street were never in danger. At the rear of Bowen-Merrill was Court Street, a generous name for what was only an alley. The buildings on the north side of Court Street were made of brick, and there were only a few windows in the rear of the Bowen-Merrill building, so these exposures were not a significant concern.

By about 4:30 p.m., firefighters were making headway. The smoke had dissipated enough for crews to reenter and fight the fire inside. Firefighters

Bowen-Merrill before the collapse. IFD's only aerial is raised to the roof with ground ladders to second floor. Hoselines and crowds of spectators can also be seen. *The Indianapolis Firefighters Museum.*

were working in the interior when, at about 5:00 p.m., the fire flared up again. Heavy smoke and flames began showing from the fourth-floor windows. IFD's only aerial truck had been placed at the front of the building, its ladder reaching the roof. A crew was on the ladder, directing a hose stream into the fourth floor. Firefighters were on Bowen-Merrill's roof playing hoselines into the skylights, and some were on ladders in the rear, bringing hoselines into the fourth floor. Firefighters were also on top of the Becker building next door to the west. Becker's was a three-story building, so the west side of Bowen-Merrill's fourth-floor wall was accessible from Becker's roof. Firefighters were trying to breach this brick wall to get water on the flames inside Bowen-Merrill's fourth floor.

THE COLLAPSE

At about 5:30 p.m., disaster struck. The crowd of spectators heard a low rumbling sound. One witness said it sounded like distant thunder. An instant later, the roof of the Bowen-Merrill building collapsed. It carried most of the fourth, third and second floors down as it fell. A tremendous roar, crashing walls and floors, breaking glass and falling debris accompanied this. Flames, smoke and steam burst from every opening. And then there was stillness.

Four reporters for the *Indianapolis News* had the best view of the collapse. They were standing on the roof of the Boston Store, the only other four-story building in that part of the block. That building was only sixty feet west of Bowen-Merrill. They watched as firefighters worked on the roof. Suddenly, they saw the men pause as they felt the first rumbling of the collapse. The firefighters quickly looked around, desperate for any avenue of escape. A few managed to make it to roofs on either side of Bowen-Merrill. However, most men went down with the roof as the reporters watched helplessly. The men fell with their arms outstretched, reaching for anything that could arrest their fall, but there was nothing. They quickly disappeared from the reporters' sight.

The four-story brick wall in the rear remained standing, unsupported. Then, it began to move back and forth, slightly at first and then gaining momentum. It finally fell inward, adding its bricks to the debris field below. More than three dozen men were on the roof and inside the building. Very few escaped death or serious injury.

The pile of rubble reached almost the height of where the second floor had been. The only part of the building that remained relatively undamaged was the cast-iron façade, along with short portions of flooring on the second, third and fourth floors still attached to the façade.

The large crowd of onlookers had a brief glimmer of hope that no serious injuries had occurred. This belief was supported as other firefighters, police and even spectators assisted the first victims from the wreckage. They were bloodied and bruised but alive. Tom Barrett was among the first rescued after he was found in Court Street covered by debris. He would survive his injuries and, in 1896, became chief of the department.

But the crowd's initial optimism faded as word spread about the many firefighters who were trapped in the wreckage.

Because the building's cast-iron façade remained standing, debris piled up behind it, sloping down and back toward the rear. Most victims were removed from the back of Bowen-Merrill, carried across Court Street and taken to a small carriage factory owned by Victor Backus. The factory, which fronted on Circle Street, was on the north side of Court Street behind Bowen-Merrill. Some doctors established a temporary hospital and morgue in the rear of the factory.

More than a dozen men were at work on the roof when the collapse occurred. Tom Dillon, a civilian, made a dramatic escape. Mr. Dillon was a foreman for the Brush Electric Light and Power Company. He was on the

A rear view of the destruction in Bowen-Merrill. The façade is standing, as is the Becker building (*right*), dating the photograph to before Wednesday afternoon, following Monday's fire. Barely visible are men searching the ruins for victims. *The Indianapolis Firefighters Museum.*

roof working with electric and telegraph lines. William Long, the Captain of Engine no. 7, and Andrew Cherry, the Superintendent of the fire alarm, were helping him. As the roof began to drop, Dillon made a desperate leap to the roof of Wasson's next door on the east. Sadly, the other two men went down in the collapse. Superintendent Cherry suffered fatal injuries, while Captain Long was seriously injured but eventually returned to duty.

The March 18, 1890 edition of the *Indianapolis Sun* quoted Tom Dillon describing what he'd seen:

> *My God! I would sooner myself go down again than set my gaze upon that terrible scene. The timbers crashed, the undermined walls and roof fell, and I could see the brave firemen with their hands aloft sinking into the awful depths. I tried to scream to Cherry and Long, but the horror of the scene made me mute. I saw Cherry stagger around frantically and Long start for the west, intending, I suppose, to leap to the Becker Building, but before he had gone half a dozen steps, the great maelstrom of debris had claimed them for its victims. As long as I live, the up-lifted hands that I saw going down to almost certain death amidst the smoke from the burning building will be a picture that my mind will retain as vividly as if it were, in all its reality, on canvas before me.*

After digging for twenty minutes, Sam Neall, the captain of Chemical Engine no. 1, was uncovered and brought out. He was injured but ironically received his most serious injury after being rescued. As two men helped Captain Neall from the building, a brick struck him in the back of the head, causing a severe wound. Some men were nearby, rescuing another victim. In their haste, one of them threw some bricks aside to uncover their victim and accidentally hit Captain Neall with one.

Thomas Black of Hook and Ladder no. 3 was the next victim found. He had not survived.

Webster "Webb" Robertson of Hose no. 5 was in the basement when the collapse occurred. Luckily, he was in an arched doorway that shielded him from most of the debris as the building fell. However, it pinned his left foot. Using his pocketknife, he cut away his left boot. That freed his foot, but it was injured, causing him pain. He limped his way through the wreckage to the rear of the basement. He called for help, and someone pulled him from the basement.

Ulysses Glazier, a twenty-three-year-old substitute firefighter, was found in the wreckage alive but with his lower body badly crushed in the debris.

His brother Peter Glazier located him in the rubble. Several men worked for over an hour to free him. Sadly, he died in his brother's arms before he was released. He was a nephew of IFD Chief Fire Engineer Daniel Glazier, who'd died in the line of duty in 1873.

George Faulkner, Engine no. 1, was rescued from beneath a pile of bricks and wood beams. He was severely injured but still alive. As he was carried into the temporary aid station and placed on a makeshift bed, he gasped once and died.

The March 19, 1890 edition of the *Indianapolis Journal* reported that David "Doc" Lowry had recently told his wife he had a feeling he might die soon. So, on Saturday, two days before the fire, he bought a $2,000 ($65,497) life insurance policy. He told his wife, "It may be foolish of me, but I brought you home a little present." He then handed her the insurance policy. Sadly, his hunch proved to be true. "Doc" Lowry, a Pipeman for Hose no. 2, did not survive the collapse.

In those days, the fire department stationed a man in a watch room high above the city to look for fires and give the alarm if one was spotted. This watch room was at the top of the clock tower of the Marion County Courthouse. There were three watchmen, and they provided the city with 24/7/365 protection.

Frank Graham was on duty in the tower on the day of the Bowen-Merrill fire. He'd watched that fire's progress while he kept an eye out for blazes in the rest of the city. Early in the evening, seeing that the smoke and flames had finally dissipated, he telephoned fire headquarters. He remarked to the man who answered the phone, "It looks like the boys have got the fire." The man gave the shocking reply, "Yes, and it got the boys! The roof fell in and killed some of them!"

By late Monday evening, the Indianapolis street commissioner had hired a crew of laborers and more than a dozen wagons to haul away debris from the fire. That would aid the search for victims.

As night fell, the Brush Electric Company set up electric lights on the roofs of nearby buildings, shining down on the wreckage, to assist the rescuers. The search for survivors continued through the night, despite constant rain. To further complicate things, the fire still burned in parts of the debris. Firefighters stood by with hoses to extinguish flames that flared up.

All but five of the known victims had been recovered by late Monday evening. Surprisingly, despite the rain, large crowds stood on Washington Street, watching the search for casualties throughout the long night.

TUESDAY, MARCH 18

William "Hickory" Jones, the driver of Chemical Engine no. 1, was located alive in the wreckage late Monday evening. A policeman tunneled into the rubble and worked several hours to free him. He finally succeeded at about 2:30 a.m. on Tuesday. At first, Hickory Jones's condition improved, but unfortunately, he died on Saturday, March 22.

John Burkhart was rescued at about 3:00 a.m. on Tuesday. He was the last firefighter removed from the wreckage alive. Sadly though, he died later that day, at 7:45 p.m.

Anthony Voltz's body was recovered on Tuesday morning at about 9:00 a.m. Despite a persistent drizzle, recovery efforts continued throughout the day, and at about 3:00 p.m., Espy Stormer's body was found. As day became night, the drizzle turned into a steady rainfall.

The exact number of missing persons was not known for sure. All of the firefighter's bodies, except for Henry Woodruff's, had been recovered. However, many spectators insisted they had seen another civilian besides Tom Dillon on the roof just before the collapse.

Due to the steady rain, officials feared some of the remaining wreckage might be dislodged and come down on the workers trying to recover victims and remove the debris. So, at about 8:15 p.m. on Tuesday, they temporarily halted the search. After almost twenty-seven hours, officials felt that any missing victims were now beyond all help.

WEDNESDAY, MARCH 19

Officials decided to bring heavy timbers to shore up parts of the Bowen-Merrill building. A portion of the second floor remained, along with remnants of other floors, all attached to the cast-iron façade.

At 8:05 a.m., alarm box no. 71 was sounded for the Fletcher Place Methodist Episcopal Church. This two-story, brick church measured about fifty by ninety feet. It was at the southeast corner of Virginia Avenue and Fletcher Street, only four blocks south and five blocks east of the Bowen-Merrill scene. Upon arrival, firefighters found heavy smoke pouring from the structure. Fire companies were working under the handicaps of exhaustion and diminished staffing due to the Bowen-Merrill tragedy. Chief Dougherty called for a second alarm at 8:09 a.m. Eventually, with these extra companies, the fire was brought under control.

The fire started in the church's basement and heavily damaged the entire building. Damage was estimated to be $4,000 ($130,993) for the building and $1,000 ($32,748) for the furnishings. Amazingly, the structure was rebuilt and continued to be used as a church for many years. Still standing, it has been converted into condominiums and is now known as the Fletcher Pointe Condos.

The first of many firefighter funerals was held on Wednesday afternoon. It was for Ulysses Grant Glazier, a twenty-three-year-old substitute firefighter.

Back at the Bowen-Merrill ruins, the work of shoring up the building was progressing when, shortly after noon, the remnants of the floors attached to the façade collapsed. Unfortunately, that also caused the collapse of much of the Becker building's east wall. More than a dozen men were working in the ruins, attempting to shore them up, while others looked for bodies. Luckily, everyone escaped safely. A few workers suffered injuries, but none were life-threatening.

After consulting with some experts, Mayor Thomas Sullivan ordered the cast-iron façade of the Bowen-Merrill building to be pulled down. It was considered dangerously weak, and there were fears that it might collapse on its own. That could put the men who were still searching the ruins for victims in danger.

The façade proved to be stronger than originally thought. Two teams of men pulling on ropes failed to bring it down. So, two windlasses, borrowed from a local company, were placed on Washington Street. Firefighters ran wire cables from the windlasses to the top of the façade. As crowds watched, the windlasses did their work, and the entire front section came down at about 4:35 p.m.

Pulling down the façade caused a partial collapse of the west wall in Wasson's Dry Goods Store, owned by Hiram P. Wasson. It also caused smoldering fires in the Bowen-Merrill wreckage to spread. Once again, box no. 45 was struck, and fire apparatus returned to the scene. Quickly spreading out of control, the flames soon threatened the Becker building to the west. It was occupied by the Housekeeper's Bargain Store, owned by Elbridge K. Bicknell. They dealt in kitchen and household furnishings. Unfortunately, much of its east wall had collapsed earlier that afternoon. That left three floors of flammable goods exposed to this new blaze. Soon, the Becker building was fully involved, and Chief Dougherty ordered a second alarm. At about 5:30 p.m., most of the Becker building collapsed, leaving just its west wall and a small portion of the rear of the building still standing. Firefighters kept the flames from spreading into George W. Sloan's

Drugstore, west of the Becker building. Sloan's did suffer some damage from the collapse next door—mainly cracks in its eastern wall and plaster falling from its ceilings and walls. Its merchandise also suffered extensive smoke damage. Chief Dougherty ordered five hose lines to play on the ruins of both buildings for the rest of the night.

THURSDAY, MARCH 20

On Thursday morning, under the mayor's direction, a committee of seven men, including architects, civil engineers and general contractors were brought together. They inspected the Wasson's building to the east of the Bowen-Merrill building and the Sloan building on the west side of the Becker building. The committee cited concerns over a partial wall collapse that had already occurred in Wasson's and the damage to Sloan's. As a result, the mayor's committee felt that both buildings should be torn down before they collapsed on their own.

The insurance companies that held the policies on these buildings threatened legal action if the buildings were razed. This matter would remain at a standstill for another day or so.

An article in the March 20, 1890 edition of the *Indianapolis Journal* reported on how exhausted the entire fire department was. The article continued, saying that fire departments throughout the Midwest knew of the tremendous loss in Indianapolis and the strain under which IFD was operating. It also said, "Quite a number of firemen from Chicago, Cincinnati, Terre Haute, Evansville, and Louisville are in town. Not to offer advice, but to be on hand to relieve the local firemen, should any give out."

Chicago was especially generous with its offers to help. Within hours of learning of the tragic loss, the Chicago Fire Department sent a representative to Indianapolis to offer any assistance the city might need. This was Chicago's way of paying back the aid that Indianapolis had once given.

In October 1871, IFD responded to a plea for help from Chicago to help fight a fire that was consuming the city. IFD sent two pumpers, two hose reels and their crews to Chicago, where they fought the fire for two days before returning home. At that time, the entire Indianapolis Fire Department consisted of only three pumpers, four hose reels and one ladder wagon. Indianapolis generously sent half its fire department 180 miles away to help Chicago. The fire apparatus and men were sent by railroad to fight what became known as the Great Chicago Fire.

On Thursday, seven funerals were held, beginning with services for David O.R. Lowry at 9:00 a.m. He was known as "Doc" and had been in the department for six and a half years. He was a Pipeman at Hose no. 2.

At 1:30 p.m., Thomas Black's funeral was held. Black was twenty-eight years old and had been a member of the IFD for two years. He was a Ladderman at Hook and Ladder no. 3, which ran out of station no. 5. His services were held next door to the station in a residence at 132 West Sixth (now Fifteenth) Street. That was the home of Black's uncle, who lived just west of Station no. 5.

In a strange coincidence, less than ten years later, that same house would be the site of another firefighter's funeral. Bowen-Merrill survivor Webster "Webb" Robertson lived in this home and worked at Station no. 5 when he died. He was driving Hose Wagon no. 5 when it was involved in an accident he didn't survive. On December 19, 1899, his funeral was held in this same home.

Another funeral was held at 1:30 p.m. on Thursday for George W. Glenn. He was a veteran of the department for fifteen years and was a Pipeman at Hose no. 10.

At 2:00 p.m., there were four separate funerals for Andrew Cherry, Albert Hoffman, Espy Stormer and Anthony Voltz.

Andrew Olin Cherry was the Superintendent of the Fire Alarm Telegraph, making him the highest-ranking IFD member to die in the tragedy. Superintendent Cherry was a sixteen-year veteran of the department and was forty-five years old.

Albert Hoffman had been in the department for six years and was a Pipeman at Hose no. 10.

Paul Espy Stormer's services were held at former IFD Chief Fire Engineer William "Decker" Sherwood's home. Espy Stormer was forty-two and was a Pipeman at Hose no. 1. He had been a member of the fire department for fifteen years. He was survived by his three children. They had been waiting for him to come home for dinner on Monday evening so they could celebrate his birthday. Instead, they learned that their father would never return home. Stormer was the children's only parent, since their mother had died in January 1887. After their father's death, the children were adopted by former chief Sherwood and his wife. The Sherwoods were the children's aunt and uncle, since Mrs. Sherwood was the late Mrs. Stormer's sister.

The final 2:00 p.m. funeral was for Anthony "Tony" Voltz. He had been in the department for seventeen years and was the driver of Hook and Ladder no. 2.

On Thursday evening, Victor Backus, who owned the carriage company that was used as a temporary hospital and morgue, made plans to look for

Henry Woodruff's body. He was motivated by his desire to bring closure to Mrs. Woodruff, who was extremely distraught because her husband's body had still not been located.

Backus and some policemen examined the ruins of the Becker building and spoke with Webb Robertson. He'd been in the basement where Woodruff was seen just before the collapse. Robertson drew a diagram to show where Woodruff's body might be. Backus and his crew decided to wait until the morning to begin their search.

FRIDAY, MARCH 21

Chief Fire Engineer Frank Dougherty, not knowing of Victor Backus's plans, announced that he would search for Woodruff's body. Bystanders urged him to reconsider, as they thought it was too dangerous. Dougherty declared he would search alone if no one wanted to help him. Learning of Dougherty's plans, Victor Backus offered the assistance of the crew he'd assembled. Thanks to Webb Robertson's diagram, they had a general idea of where Woodruff's body might be and began digging a tunnel through the debris toward that area. While most of the crewmen worked in the rubble, two men intently watched the walls on either side of the ruins. They were looking for any sign of movement, which might indicate a collapse. Police kept spectators at least two hundred feet from the buildings to minimize the vibrations they might cause.

Finally, at about 4:30 p.m., the searchers uncovered one of Woodruff's legs. They carefully dug out his lower body, but heavy timbers and other debris still trapped the upper portion. After working for another hour, Woodruff's body was finally recovered from the ruins. It had taken four days of searching to find it.

Since no civilian bodies were found and no one was reported missing, authorities were confident that all human remains had now been recovered. With the search for bodies over, the mayor decided to take no further action in tearing down the Sloan and Wasson buildings. Instead, city officials gave control of those damaged buildings back to their owners and let them and their insurance companies decide what to do with them.

Two more funerals took place on Friday afternoon. The first was for John S. Burkhart. He was a substitute firefighter working that fateful day for Thomas Quinn of Engine no. 1.

The other funeral, held on Friday, was for George S. "Deacon" Faulkner, a sixteen-year veteran. He was the Engineer on Engine no. 1.

SATURDAY, MARCH 22

William Jones, known as "Hickory," died this morning, at a little after 9:00 a.m. He had been trapped in the wreckage for about ten hours before he was rescued early on Tuesday morning. Rescuers took him to his home to recover. He felt well enough to give newspaper interviews on Wednesday and Thursday but took a turn for the worse on Friday. He was the twelfth firefighter to die since the fire started on Monday.

Henry David Woodruff's funeral was held at 2:00 p.m. on Saturday. His had been the last body taken from the wreckage. Woodruff was a nineteen-year veteran of IFD and was a Pipeman for Hose no. 5.

SUNDAY, MARCH 23

Ministers in churches throughout Indianapolis gave sermons praising the firefighters and lamenting their deaths and injuries. Many churches also held special collections to add to the donations already being collected for the fallen firefighters.

At 3:00 p.m. on Sunday, a memorial service was held for the firefighters. Mayor Thomas Sullivan, the city council and other city officials were all in attendance, as was an estimated crowd of four thousand. The service took place in Tomlinson Hall.

Later on Sunday evening, the first of several concerts given to raise money for the families of the firefighters who were lost and injured was held. It also occurred in Tomlinson Hall.

MONDAY, MARCH 24

The final funeral in a long, terrible week occurred on Monday, March 24. It was for William F. "Hickory" Jones, who had been in the department for less than a year. He was the driver of Chemical Engine no. 1. Jones and his wife were from Fillmore, Putnam County, Indiana. He was buried in the Fillmore Cemetery. On Monday morning, the president of the St. Louis, Vandalia and Terre Haute Railroad furnished a private railroad car to take the casket and mourners to Fillmore for the funeral and burial.

THE AFTERMATH

Beyond the tragic deaths and injuries, the damage was estimated at $135,000 ($4,421,027) for the Bowen-Merrill building and its stock of books and other goods; $10,000 ($327,484) for the Becker building; and $8,000 ($261,987) for the Housekeeper's Bargain Store stock. The loss of the Wasson building was about $25,000 ($818,709), with another $25,000 ($818,709) for its damaged merchandise. This meant the total damages were at least $203,000 ($6,647,915). This figure does not include the damage suffered by Sloan's Drugstore and smoke and water damage sustained by nearby stores.

There was a tremendous outpouring of monetary donations to aid the firefighters and their families. In that era, Indianapolis had several newspapers. By the end of the week following the fire, almost $20,000 ($654,967) had been donated to the various newspaper firefighter relief funds.

Over the weeks and months following the tragedy, there were many benefit fundraisers, such as concerts and dances, held, with the proceeds going to the relief fund.

The president of the United States at the time, Benjamin Harrison, and his wife, Caroline, sent a personal donation of $200 ($6,549). They had resided in Indianapolis before his election and considered it their home. A group of former Indianapolis residents now living in Washington, D.C., donated $400 ($13,099). In addition, many fire departments inside and outside of Indiana sent monetary donations and expressions of sympathy. Many firefighters and fire officials from outside departments also attended the funerals.

On May 30, 1890, the citizens' committee met and reported on how the money from the Firemen's Relief Fund would be distributed. A total of $51,938.96 ($1,700,915.33) had been donated.

The committee said that $3,146.02 ($103,026.97) was spent on funeral expenses and temporary relief for the families of the deceased firefighters. In addition, the fund paid medical costs totaling $1,621.20 ($53,091.63) for the injured firefighters.

The relief fund allowed each of the nine widows to have their existing home mortgages paid off or, if they had previously rented homes, to have residences purchased for them. It also provided an annuity of $180 ($5,895) per year for each widow for the rest of her life. In addition, each child who lost their father would receive $60 ($1,965) per year until they reached the age of sixteen.

The general public had been very generous with their monetary donations to the firefighters. However, Indianapolis city and fire department officials knew a more permanent solution was needed. Establishing a pension would ensure there would be money to compensate for the firefighters' deaths and injuries. It would also enable firefighters to retire as they get older.

In an effort between Indiana state legislators and insurance company officials, a pension plan was announced. Insurance companies and contributions from individual firefighters would fund it. It went into effect on June 1, 1891.

Ultimately, twelve men either died the day of the fire or within the five days following the fire. A thirteenth victim, William Raper McGinnis, died of his injuries less than three years later. McGinnis had been the Captain of Hose no. 8. He and two other members of Hose no. 8 were operating a hose line on the third floor when the collapse occurred. A small part of the floor remained, still attached to the façade, and luckily, the three men remained on this portion of the third floor after the collapse. However, William McGinnis was very close to the edge and slid down the hose to the debris field below to escape. While doing this, he somehow injured his spine. The injury seemed minor at first. But in the following months, his condition worsened. Eventually, he was placed on light duty. In August 1891, the injury forced him to retire. By December 1892, his situation had deteriorated, and he needed an operation on his spine. The surgery was performed on December 20, and McGinnis was reportedly recovering. Unfortunately, complications set in on December 22, 1892, and he died that evening. He had been a firefighter just short of thirteen years when he was forced to retire in 1891. William McGinnis's funeral was held on December 26, 1892.

In March 1890, the Indianapolis Fire Department had six pumper companies, ten hose companies, two chemical engines, two city service ladder trucks and one aerial ladder truck. Between eighty-two and eighty-nine men manned this apparatus. Reports vary on the actual number of men on the roster at that time. But using either number, with twenty-eight firefighters either killed or seriously injured, about one-third of the total number of firefighters in IFD were affected by the Bowen-Merrill fire. Of the department's twenty-one companies, only six had no deaths or serious injuries within their ranks.

Two of the men killed were substituting for full-time firefighters who wanted a day off. Since both substitutes worked for other firefighters, those two positions did not need replacements. However, that left twenty-six slots within the department that quickly needed replacements. The captain of each fire company hired the men they needed to replace the firefighters lost in their company. Chief Frank Dougherty then had the final say about who was employed.

The coroner began an inquest two days after the fire. One of the topics regarded the fire chief and his handling of the fire. A local newspaper printed rumors that the firefighters lacked confidence in Chief Dougherty. They also said that some firefighters had refused direct orders from the chief, hampering the firefighting efforts.

The inquest lasted several days, while members of the fire department, employees of Bowen-Merrill, construction workers and even Silas Bowen, who owned both the business and the building, testified.

One carpenter testified that he'd previously worked on the building. He said that he'd dug down to the foundation in part of the basement. He believed the foundation he uncovered was inadequate for the brick walls it supported. He felt so strongly about this unsafe foundation that he quit and refused to work there any longer.

Another witness, an employee of the bookstore, gave testimony about a conversation he'd overheard in 1872. He said he'd heard a workman who was installing an elevator exclaim to another worker, "Great God! I don't see how this building stands with the foundation that it has under it!"

On March 26, 1890, Coroner Theodore Wagner gave his final verdict on the deaths of the twelve (at that time) firefighters. His findings showed that the building (actually two combined buildings) had been modified several times since it was first constructed. It had changed from the original two- and three-story heights to an entire four-story building still on the original foundation. That 1840s foundation was never intended or designed to support a structure of the height and weight the Bowen-Merrill building had become.

The coroner stated that the fire, even though it started the tragic event, did not cause the collapse. He said, "The fire was not of itself sufficient to cause the collapse." Continuing his verdict, he simply said, "I find that the building was of faulty construction." However, he did not say who might be responsible for causing this condition.

So, who was responsible? Was it the architect (if there was one) who designed the additional stories? Was it the builder of the additional floors? Was it Mr. Bowen, who ordered the construction? After more than 130 years, it's still difficult to adequately place blame.

Coroner Wagner had this to say about Chief Frank Dougherty's leadership and the fire department's activities during the fire: "The testimony is unanimous that the fire department, from chief to firefighters, acted promptly and intelligently. I find that the chief has the fullest confidence of his men and that he, and they, deserve the commendation of the community."

In conclusion, the coroner said, "To prevent further calamities, I recommend the appointment of a competent building inspector."

That finally happened when Michael Fitchey, a former Chief Fire Engineer of the Indianapolis Fire Department, was appointed the city's first building inspector in April 1891.

Contractors had cleared the sites of the damaged buildings by May 1890, and construction immediately started on the two buildings that were set to replace them. They were completed in a remarkably short time. Just five months later, on October 14, 1890, a new structure opened on the site that was previously occupied by both Wasson's and Bowen-Merrill's stores. It was the new four-story H.P. Wasson Dry Goods Store at 12–18 West Washington Street. Next door, on Wasson's west side, was the new Becker building. Its address was 20 West Washington Street.

Also opening in October was the new location of Bowen-Merrill and Company's bookstore at 9 and 11 West Washington Street. It was in a remodeled building on the south side of Washington Street, almost directly across from its previous location.

In 1937, the third Wasson building was torn down so that H.P. Wasson and Company could build an even larger store. That building still stands on the northwest corner of Washington and Meridian Streets. Its footprint covers the sites of both the third Wasson building and four other buildings once located east of the third Wasson building. The National Park Service placed the fourth Wasson building in its National Register of Historic Places in 1997.

ADDITIONAL VICTIMS OF THE FIRE

William Partee and Samuel Null, who were both injured at Bowen-Merrill, quit the fire department within a few years. Their reasons for doing so are not known. Department records only indicate that the men resigned. Whether their decision was related to what they experienced on that terrible day is unknown. William Partee suffered serious injuries as he went down with the roof. He resigned in December 1892. Samuel Null was not injured in the collapse but suffered injuries while assisting with rescue operations. He left in November 1893.

Louis Rafert, a Pipeman from Engine no. 3, was one of the forgotten victims of the fire. He was working on the roof when it collapsed. Rafert was buried in the debris, unable to call for help. Rescuers took him from the rubble, and he was hospitalized for several weeks before being released. He returned to his job with the 3s, but four years later, he was given a light-duty job. Rafert did this job for a few years before his health forced him to request a disability retirement in 1896. Then in 1898, he was reinstated to the department and given a light-duty job. He had been on the job again for only two months before he asked to be retired for a final time. On April 7, 1903, Louis Frederick Rafert died of tuberculosis. The disease may have developed due to his exposure to the elements while awaiting rescue in the collapse debris. Louis Rafert was thirty-seven years old. His funeral was held on April 9, 1903.

Another forgotten victim whose death was the result from his injuries in the fire was Albert Meurer. He was the Captain of Truck no. 2 at the time of the incident. He suffered severe head injuries in the collapse. He returned to work after several months, but other firefighters said he sometimes acted strangely. He retired in June 1899, nine years after the fire. He had served for twenty-six years at that time. In 1901, he was arrested after threatening to harm his family. Following a trial, he was found mentally ill and sent to Central State Hospital for the Insane. He died there on March 21, 1904. At the time, he was being treated for paresis, a muscle weakness or paralysis. One cause of paresis can be a brain injury. Albert Coval Meurer was fifty-six at the time of his death. His funeral took place on March 24, 1904.

Yet another victim, although his was not considered a line of duty death, was Frank Harvey. He was the Captain of Truck no. 1 and had been in the department since 1882. Wanting to take a day off, he'd hired Ulysses Glazier to take his place. When Harvey learned of the blaze, he hurried to the scene and was fighting fire when the collapse occurred. Captain Harvey was uninjured. Later, he witnessed Glazier's body being taken from the wreckage. The realization that Glazier only worked that day so he could have a day off greatly affected Captain Harvey. He remained on duty but constantly talked about how he felt personally responsible for Glazier's death. Frank Harvey was also remorseful because he was unmarried while Glazier was married and had a young child. On December 22, 1892, William McGinnis died from his injuries. After learning of McGinnis's death, Harvey became even more despondent and stopped eating. He grew weaker and had to be hospitalized. Early on the morning of January 6, 1893, while in the hospital, he hanged himself with a bedsheet. Frank W. Harvey was thirty-eight years old. His funeral was held on January 9, 1893.

Another sad chapter in this terrible saga was that of Charles Jenkins. He was the driver of Hose no. 5 and had only been with the IFD since July 1889. The day of the fire was his regular day off. After hearing about the fire, he responded to the scene, where Chief Dougherty told him to assist wherever he could. He went to the rear of the building and helped take a hose into the basement. Jenkins then climbed a ladder to the third floor. Seeing how much fire was up there, he began climbing down, intending to return with a hose. He'd gone down only a few rungs when the collapse occurred. Jenkins fell backward, landing on his back in Court Street. As he landed, bricks struck him on the head, dazing him. After staggering to his feet, he began unsteadily walking down Court Street. A bystander helped him to Sloan's Drugstore for treatment for his injuries.

Charles Jenkins wasn't badly injured and was soon back at work. However, on April 13, 1891, he didn't return to duty following his regular day off. His family reported him missing. Many rumors began spreading about him. People whispered that he was heavily in debt. Some persons speculated that he'd left town to avoid his obligations. Others thought that Jenkins had possibly met with foul play because of the money he owed. Still others feared that he might have been contemplating death by suicide. Whatever the reason, Charles Jenkins was never seen again in Indianapolis. When he disappeared, he left behind his wife and two young children.

The Bowen-Merrill fire also weighed heavily on Sam Neall, the Captain of Chemical Engine no. 1. Neall received serious injuries in the fire. However, an article in the *Indianapolis Journal* on May 15, 1892, told of his feelings about the death of William "Hickory" Jones: "I can't get away from the idea that I was indirectly the cause of that fellow's death, and thoughts of him seem to haunt me at times and stare me in the face when I am least expecting them."

A few days before the fire, Jones, the driver of Chemical Engine no. 1, mentioned that he would not be working on Monday, telling Neall that he had hired a substitute. Captain Neall told him, "Jones, you had better save that money by working for yourself." Jones thought about it and then telephoned the substitute, telling him not to come in—he would be working his own shift, after all. Unfortunately, "Hickory" Jones was caught in the collapse and died the following Saturday. Samuel Neall retired on disability in December 1896 and was reinstated in April 1899. He served until he retired again on March 10, 1914. He died on July 5, 1919, still bothered by Jones's death.

The third victim, forgotten for so long, was William Hinesley. He died on June 7, 1914, from injuries he'd suffered twenty-four years previously.

He'd been on the roof of the Bowen-Merrill building when the collapse occurred. Hinesley was seriously injured but, after seven months, was able to return to duty. After his recovery, he was promoted to Engineer of Engine no. 1. William Hinesley retired in January 1897, and in 1914, he became the sixteenth and final firefighter to die from injuries caused by the Bowen-Merrill fire. His funeral was held on June 9, 1914.

All the firefighters who survived this disaster possessed their own memories of the tragedy. Each of them dealt with these memories in different ways. Most of them lived with what they had seen and done on that awful day and didn't let it adversely affect their lives. However, other survivors had more difficulty in processing what they'd experienced. One of them took his own life. Another disappeared, leaving his family behind. At least two others quit the department within a few years of the incident. Yet another felt guilt for the rest of his life because he felt responsible for one of the firefighters who didn't survive.

All these incidents may have been caused by what we know today as post-traumatic stress disorder (PTSD). First responders suffer from PTSD more often than people in many other occupations.

8

THE SURGICAL INSTITUTE FIRE

J ust before midnight on Thursday, January 21, 1892, a horrific fire killed nineteen men, women and children in downtown Indianapolis. The victims were patients and, in some cases, their relatives, in a private hospital called the National Surgical Institute of Indianapolis.

Dr. Horace Allen founded the hospital in Charleston, Illinois, in 1858. It was known as the Surgical Institute. In 1869, he and Dr. William Johnson moved the practice to Indianapolis, and the facility became the Indiana Surgical Institute. The name changed again in 1872 to become the National Surgical Institute of Indianapolis.

The institute treated patients with orthopedic problems, such as bone deformities, rheumatism and hip, joint and spinal problems. They performed surgical procedures and fitted braces and crutches that were custom made for patients. The hospital was one of the only medical facilities in the country that specialized in orthopedic procedures. Because of this, people across the country came to Indianapolis for treatment. Patients ranged from very young infants to older adults.

The institute occupied three buildings. The main hospital was a four-story, brick, 65-by-100-foot structure on the northeast corner of Illinois and Georgia Streets. Since the building was on the corner, it had 65 feet of frontage on Illinois Street and 100 feet on Georgia Street. Adjoining that building to the north was a three-story brick building on Illinois Street. It measured 50 by 65 feet and was known as the North Annex. Finally, to the east of the main hospital, on the north side of Georgia Street, was

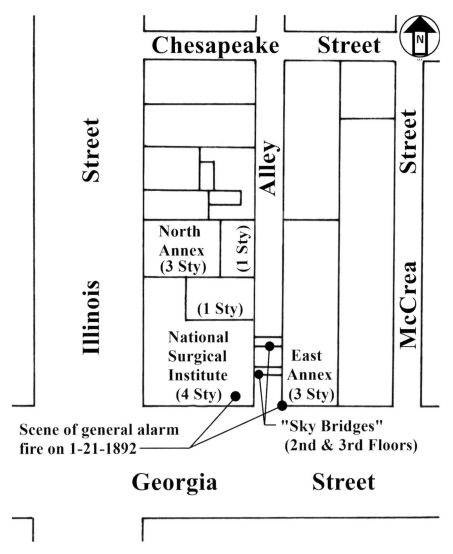

A map showing the area of the Surgical Institute fire. Although they had been given names, McCrea and Chesapeake Streets were alleys. The other alley was not named. *Map by author.*

a three-story brick building. That structure measured 55 by 115 feet and was known as the East Annex. A one-story, 55-by-90-foot building with a flat roof adjoined the East Annex on its north side. On its east side was a three-story, 60-by-175-foot warehouse. These structures were not part of the hospital.

The two buildings on Illinois Street shared a common wall. In addition, the East Annex on Georgia Street was connected to the main hospital building by two enclosed wooden walkways on the second and third floors. These sky bridges were necessary due to an alley that ran north and south and separated the two buildings. All the hospital structures were once hotels.

The ground floors of the main hospital and the North Annex had several retail establishments. These businesses had nothing to do with the hospital. The upper floors of the two buildings were mainly used to house patient rooms. Of the seventy-two rooms on these floors, sixty-five were reserved for patients, while the rest were for employees.

All three floors of the Georgia Street building were devoted to the hospital. The ground floor had offices, a lecture hall and treatment and operating rooms. There was a dining room, recreation area and additional offices on the second floor. Ten patient rooms and three employee sleeping rooms were on the third floor.

No fire escapes were installed on the outside of the buildings, as was common in many multistory buildings at the time. The East Annex did have a single metal ladder mounted to the front of the structure. It extended from the sidewalk to the roof. However, using this ladder proved challenging during the fire because of flames, heat and smoke pouring from the structure.

Instead, what was provided for fire escapes were ropes. These ropes were attached to the wall below each window and coiled in a box. In case of fire, the occupants would open the window, throw the free end of the rope to the sidewalk and then climb down to safety. That might work well for a healthy person, but what about those with disabilities? After all, this was a hospital for people with orthopedic problems. And what of the very young or older adults? Would they be able to climb down a rope from a room as high as the fourth floor without assistance? This type of fire escape left much to be desired, especially in a hospital.

The fire began in an office on the first floor of the East Annex building. Exactly what started it was never determined. The temperature was cold, with daytime highs in the upper thirties. That night was just below freezing with some snow flurries.

At about 11:40 p.m. on January 21, 1892, while patrolling in the building, George Finn, the night watchman, heard what he described as a "crackling noise" in the brochure room. He discovered a shelf stacked with paper goods on fire when he opened the door. He immediately ran to the third-floor room of John Wilson, the night supervisor, to let him know of the situation. Then the watchman returned downstairs and ran outside to the

FROM THE GEORGIA-STREET FRONT.

An illustration from the *Indianapolis Journal* showing the main hospital (*left*) and the East Annex (*right*) at the height of the fire. *Courtesy of the* Indianapolis Journal.

nearest alarm box at the corner of Meridian and Georgia Streets. He turned in the alarm from box no. 92 and returned to the stricken building. The first alarm was transmitted at 11:45 p.m.

In the meantime, Mr. Wilson, the supervisor, went to the brochure room and found the fire had spread to a wall of shelves loaded with paper goods. He left the room to telephone the fire department. Upon returning with a fire extinguisher, he found that the fire now involved the entire room and was spreading into an adjoining office and hallway. He quickly realized that this was beyond anything he could control with an extinguisher. He and the watchman then ran through the buildings, pounding on doors and shouting to awaken the patients.

After receiving the alarm, Hose Wagon no. 7, responding from its station on Maryland Street, east of Meridian Street, was the first apparatus on the scene. The January 23, 1892 edition of the *Indianapolis Journal* quoted Captain Jim Campbell of the hose company: "We came to a stop at Georgia Street, on Meridian [alarm box no. 92 was on that corner], unable to see where the fire was. We were about to turn east on Georgia Street when I saw some women running across the street to the west in their nightclothes. 'For Christ's sake,' I said to the driver, 'hurry to the west; it's the Surgical institute!'" He yelled to the aerial ladder, which had responded from the same station, to follow them. He told the newspaper that his company made it to the second floor with a hose line within about two minutes. However, they did not throw any water because of all the people. "We had to drop the hose and pay our whole attention to rescuing the people," Campbell explained. "We could see the full length of the hallway. It was a seething furnace of flames!"

The fire crews were greeted with the awful specter of a rapidly spreading fire, heavy smoke and many helpless victims awaiting rescue. Fire was already showing from windows on all three floors of the East Annex. People were at some of the windows screaming for help.

Chief Fire Engineer Joseph Webster arrived and, seeing the extreme life safety risk, immediately called for a second alarm. A third alarm quickly followed, and then came a general alarm bringing the city's entire fire force to the scene. Very quickly, all efforts were directed toward lifesaving. Every ladder was placed against the buildings, and many rescues were performed this way.

Unfortunately, some victims didn't wait for rescue. Early in the incident, firefighters saw a woman and a young child at a window on the third floor of the East Annex. The room behind them was bright with flames as the woman screamed for help. Holding the child close, she threatened to jump from the window. Firefighters pleaded with her to await rescue. However, the heat and smoke were becoming unbearable. Finally, Delia Lazarus made the awful decision that she could wait no longer. Gathering her seven-year-old daughter, Lottie, in her arms, she climbed onto the windowsill. She could hear the firefighters below shouting at her to stay there and wait for them. But it was just too hot. She stepped off the sill.

The unfortunate pair landed almost at the feet of firefighters who were preparing to rescue them and other victims. Ultimately, their three-story jump cost them their lives. They'd both suffered burns before jumping and were gravely injured by the fall. The mother died two hours later, while the young girl clung to life until Saturday evening before succumbing to her injuries.

The Lazarus family was from Dallas, Texas, and Samuel Lazarus, the husband and father, was a clothing company salesman. He was in Philadelphia on business when he heard about the fire. Mr. Lazarus saw a newspaper headline describing a large fire in Indianapolis with many fatalities. Knowing his wife and daughter were there, he grabbed the paper and read the terrible news. The article told of how his loved ones had jumped and that both were seriously injured. Later, when Mr. Lazarus learned that his wife had died and his daughter wasn't expected to live, the news overwhelmed him, and he fainted. He took the first available train to Indianapolis and was able to spend time with his young daughter before she died.

Mrs. Lazarus's brother Frank Beard was a telegraph operator in Chicago. He was working that night and noticed many telegrams coming from Indianapolis. They all had a similar message: "Institute burned. I am safe." He telegraphed the Indianapolis operator and asked, "What institute is burning?" "The National Surgical Institute" was the reply. The Chicago operator immediately telegraphed that he had a sister and niece at the institute and asked the operator if they had heard any news of Mrs. Lazarus or her daughter. After checking with officials, he had to telegraph Mr. Beard the unfortunate news that his sister had died and that his niece wasn't expected to survive.

Meanwhile, successful rescues were being made. John Loucks of Chemical Engine no. 2 was on a ladder at a fourth-floor window. The Captain of Chemical Engine no. 2, John Robinson, handed him a small child that he'd found in one of the rooms. Loucks began to descend the ladder while holding the child, but his foot slipped on an icy rung. He fell a few feet, but luckily, his leg caught on a rung and stopped him from falling down completely. He was left near the top, dangling and hanging upside down by one leg. But he managed to hold onto the child. Other firefighters saw what had happened and climbed up to help him. One firefighter brought the child down safely while others assisted Loucks, who had suffered ankle and hip injuries but no broken bones. John Loucks would serve as IFD's chief from 1918 to 1922.

Firefighter John Costello of Hose no. 10 caught a baby who was dropped from the third floor by their desperate mother while he stood on the sidewalk. Other firefighters rescued the mother, who was later reunited with her child.

Simeon Hoyle, a substitute firefighter, made it up to the fourth floor of the main building, where he found an unconscious woman. The room she was in was already heavily engulfed in flame, but Hoyle managed to carry her downstairs through the heat and smoke. She suffered burns on her feet and legs but survived.

Sergeant John Lowe of the Indianapolis Police Department made it up to the third floor of the East Annex. He found a woman and her baby in a room. He carried the child, telling the woman to follow him. Reaching the second-floor landing, they were suddenly overwhelmed by heat and smoke. The woman panicked and jumped over the railing to the first floor. She was not injured. Still holding the baby, Sergeant Lowe continued down the stairs but became blinded by the smoke. He fell down the stairway but never let go of the child. Neither he nor the baby was injured. The woman and her child were reunited outside.

A FIREMAN'S LUCKY CATCH.

An illustration from the *Indianapolis News* showing firefighter John Costello catching a baby who was dropped from the third floor by their mother. Both the mother and child survived. *Courtesy of the* Indianapolis News.

One of the highlights of an otherwise horrible night were the actions of Mrs. Thompson, who was in charge of the institute's nursery. The nursery was on the top floor of the main building. It was holding forty-three children, all asleep, when the fire broke out. These were children whose parents couldn't remain with them and had to leave them in the care of the institute during their treatment. Mrs. Thompson smelled smoke and heard shouting early in the fire. Unfortunately, the only exit from the nursery was a nearby stairway. The problem was that the stairway had a gate, and she and the children were locked behind it for security reasons. The gate was made of one-eighth-inch-thick wire grating, and Mrs. Thompson had no key. She also had no tools to force open or cut the grate. She finally resorted to tearing away the heavy grating with her bare hands. Mrs. Thompson badly cut her hands while doing this but finally opened the gate. Despite her pain, she ran downstairs to get help for the children. She then returned to the nursery, bringing back several police officers. Mrs. Thompson, assisted by the officers, managed to get all forty-three children to safety. Not a single child from the nursery was injured.

Mrs. Thompson was a heroine, but no one bothered to print her first name in any newspaper articles. Unfortunately, a search of newspapers and city directories from that era failed to disclose conclusively what her full name may have been.

Meanwhile, smoke and flames in the East Annex had quickly spread through the sky bridges into the main building on the corner of Illinois and Georgia Streets. It was speculated that had the sky bridges been built of metal instead of wood, the fire could've been contained to the East Annex. But instead, it spread into the main hospital after the sky bridges caught fire.

That building's roof and fourth floor were severely damaged. The lower floors suffered smoke and water damage, but most of the fire was on the fourth floor. The warehouse east of the East Annex was undamaged by fire.

The North Annex building, which adjoined the main hospital on its north side, was not damaged in the incident. Closed doors kept the fire, and much of the smoke, out of that building.

Over three hundred patients and their relatives were in the hospital at the time of the fire. In addition, there were about thirty employees, such as doctors, nurses and orderlies present.

The final death toll was nineteen, with victims ranging in age from three to sixty-five. Eight victims were in rooms on the third floor of the East Annex, and nine more died in rooms on the fourth floor of the main hospital building. The remaining fatalities comprised the woman who'd jumped while holding her daughter.

Dozens of people were injured, with at least twenty-four seriously hurt. Their injuries ranged from severe burns, broken bones and internal injuries to smoke inhalation, cuts and bruises. All the deaths and many injuries occurred to people who lived outside Indiana. They'd traveled to Indianapolis to get help for their medical conditions. But instead of relief, they became victims of a terrible disaster.

Once the fire was out, the search for victims began. Initially, there were many rumors about the number of people who'd died in the fire. Some firefighters estimated that fifty or more bodies might be in the debris. One unidentified firefighter was quoted in a newspaper as saying that he'd seen numerous piles of white ashes in the buildings. He claimed that each of these piles were the remains of a person the fire had entirely consumed. Fortunately, his theory was false. However, two days after the fire, newspapers reported that many additional victims were expected to be found in the rubble. Part of the problem was that, as people fled the fire or were rescued, they were taken to various locations. Unfortunately, there was no system to track the survivors' locations, so no one knew exactly how many patients might be missing.

Some of the injured went to a makeshift hospital in a nearby hotel. Other victims were at St. Vincents Hospital, which, in those days, was on South Street, just a few blocks from the fire scene. Concerned neighbors also opened their homes and apartments to help survivors escape the cold weather. As a result, hospital patients were scattered all over the city, regardless of whether they were injured.

Another problem was that the fire destroyed the ledger that listed all the patients in the hospital. It took several days to assemble another list of everyone who was being treated in the hospital that night. Once that was compiled, a comparison with a list of the patients already accounted for revealed only two missing patients. That was remarkable, given the chaos the night of the fire. One missing patient was located with a nearby family. Her name was added to the survivors' list.

That left just one missing person, a five-year-old boy named Arthur Bayles. He'd been in the hospital while his mother stayed with him. Then a few days earlier, she had to return to her home in Wisconsin to care for her other children. Her husband became ill and could no longer care for the children, as he'd been doing. So, she left her son in the care of Mrs. J.R. Guild, a woman with a young daughter, in the hospital. Officials couldn't interview Mrs. Guild about the missing boy because she'd been injured while she was being rescued and was unconscious until Saturday morning. When Mrs. Guild regained consciousness, officials asked about the young boy who was left in her care. She told them Arthur Bayles had been with her and her daughter when firefighters came in through a window to rescue them.

Tragically, it turned out that he'd been left behind during all the chaos and confusion. Just moments after being helped out the window, Mrs. Guild fell from the ladder and was knocked unconscious after hitting the sidewalk. She couldn't tell firefighters a young boy was still in her room. Mrs. Guild's daughter was only three, and due to her young age, she didn't know to tell anyone about the boy. He hadn't cried out, or if he did, firefighters hadn't heard him. So, they unknowingly left him to his fate.

Armed with this new information, firefighters searched Mrs. Guild's room. Arthur Bayles's remains were found under a pile of debris. His body was recovered on Saturday morning. The five-year-old child was the last victim found in the ruins. Luckily, the rumors about many additional victims were untrue.

The day after the fire, controversy erupted when Dr. Allen announced his plans to rebuild the damaged buildings and continue business at the tragic site. Charles Reynolds, a representative for Dr. Allen, applied for a building permit to "rebuild and repair the Surgical Institute." It stated that "the rebuilding would be done under the control and direction of Michael Fitchey, the Indianapolis Building Inspector." Fitchey, a former IFD Chief Fire Engineer, quickly disavowed any connection with the project.

Newspaper editorials came out strongly against this proposal. For example, one in the January 23, 1892 edition of the *Indianapolis Journal* called the idea "objectionable on humanitarian and hygienic grounds." It also stated that "a new institute should be located in a suburban area, or at least somewhere where there is an abundance of fresh air and a glimpse of green earth."

A letter signed by "A.O.M." in the January 24, 1892 edition of the *Indianapolis Journal* included a rather insensitive statement. That person wrote, "Why shouldn't the city authorities regulate this matter and compel the doctor to build his new institution out on the edge of the city, where every visiting stranger will not think that Indianapolis is a swarm of cripples and paralytics?"

That statement referenced the hospital's patients, who often congregated on sidewalks in front of the buildings during nice weather. The institute was just one block north of Union Station. Many of the city's visitors would pass by these patients sunning themselves on the sidewalks as they walked from the railroad station to their hotels. The letter writer felt that seeing these patients, many of whom suffered from obvious physical disabilities, might give out-of-town visitors a bad impression of Indianapolis.

On Saturday, probably sensing that public opinion was turning against him and the institute, Dr. Allen issued a statement: "To our friends, we wish to state that the rumors of our rebuilding on the present site for institute purposes is unfounded, such is not our intention." He said the institute had decided to "build a sufficient number of cottages on a large piece of ground, quite a distance from the business portion of the city." This plan did not come to pass either. As will be seen, when the new hospital opened, it was built as one structure, not a "number of cottages," as Dr. Allen had stated. Further, it was on the west side of the downtown area, not "quite a distance from the business portion of the city."

Frank Manker, the Marion County coroner, investigated the fire. This inquest lasted almost a month and saw 197 people interviewed. Testimony by hospital employees and patients showed that many victims required walking assistance. A lot of them needed braces or crutches to get around. Survivors testified that there was plenty of time to escape. The problem was that many patients panicked, and some refused to leave their rooms until they were fully dressed. Others took the time to gather their valuables. Unfortunately, these actions sometimes resulted in death or injury.

The coroner ruled that seventeen victims had died of suffocation from the heavy smoke. They were found in rooms on the top floors of the main hospital and the East Annex. The remaining victims—the mother and her young daughter—died of extensive injuries after they jumped from a third-floor window. Coroner Manker contended that the deaths of all nineteen victims resulted from "fright, confusion of mind, and the awful suddenness with which the disaster came upon them."

In the end, the coroner ruled that "the buildings occupied by the National Surgical Institute were well provided with exits, fire escapes and facilities for fighting a fire, and as safe as such buildings are, which are not fireproof."

This verdict was rather shocking, especially given an article published in the October 25, 1878 edition of the *Indianapolis News*. It said that John Pendergrast, then IFD's Chief Fire Engineer, and several of his most experienced men inspected many public buildings, such as hotels, hospitals and apartments, to ascertain their safety. The chief said this about the National Surgical Institute: "The Surgical Institute is hardly a satisfactory building, from a fireman's point of view. The stairways are narrow, crooked, and of insufficient number; the halls are dark and winding, and even at midday, one stumbles through them, feeling his way as if blindfolded." In another part of the article was this prediction, which was sadly prophetic: "Everything about the building invites fire, and if it comes, there will be a loss of human life, as on the upper floors are numbers of cripples who would be unable to escape, even with more favorable surroundings." Remember, Chief Pendergrast said this more than thirteen years before the tragic 1892 fire.

Former Chief John Pendergast was interviewed again following the 1892 fire. He reiterated what was found in 1878: "It was the worst death trap I ever saw in Indianapolis!"

Generally speaking, the public disliked the coroner's verdict. They felt the Surgical Institute's owners should have shouldered more responsibility for the deaths and injuries. There were also questions about the general safety of the buildings. How could the coroner rule that the buildings were safe and that fire protection within them was adequate compared with the 1878 report on the facility? There had been no substantial improvements to safety in the intervening years.

Coroner Frank Manker ran for reelection in November 1892. Possibly due to voters' concerns about his verdict on the Surgical Institute fire, he lost his bid for another term.

The property loss in this fire totaled about $25,000 ($818,709). The East Annex on Georgia Street was severely damaged by the fire and razed a few weeks later. The damaged main hospital building and the relatively undamaged North Annex were sold after the fire. Their damage was repaired, and they both became hotels again. Various businesses continued using these buildings at least until the 1960s.

In February 1894, the National Surgical Institute of Indianapolis completed the construction of a new four-story hospital on the northwest corner of Ohio Street and Capitol Avenue. That was immediately north of the state capitol building. Unfortunately, due in part to the high construction costs of the new building, they were forced to raise their fees. These increased prices caused patients to seek other medical facilities, and the National Surgical Institute eventually ceased operations in Indianapolis and sold its building. That newer hospital later became a hotel. It was torn down in the late 1940s, and the second hospital site is now a parking lot.

Today, the site of the Surgical Institute's three buildings on Illinois and Georgia Streets is covered by part of the Circle Centre Mall. But sadly, there is no marker or memorial to remember the nineteen lives lost on that tragic night.

9

THE BROAD RIPPLE NATURAL GAS EXPLOSIONS

On the morning of September 4, 1897, the small suburban Indianapolis town of Broad Ripple was rocked by two large explosions and subsequent fires. Seven men died in the wreckage of a grocery store. Many others sustained injuries ranging from minor to very serious. At that time, Broad Ripple was a separate town located a few miles north of Indianapolis. In 1922, it was annexed and became a part of the city of Indianapolis.

September 4 began as a quiet Saturday morning in Broad Ripple. Watts' Drug Store stood on the northeast corner of Main Street and Cherry Street (now Guilford Avenue). It was on the ground floor of a two-story, wood-frame building with a basement. The second floor was the home of the Broad Ripple Christian Church. The church had recently sold its building and moved to this new location.

James Watts, the drugstore's owner, and his three sons, Edgar, Frank and James Jr., were inside the store that morning. Also present were Emsley Johnson and Tyson Mitchener. At about 9:30 a.m., Edgar Watts was teaching his friend, Emsley Johnson, how to develop photographs. Edgar had a small darkroom that he'd built in the rear storeroom of the drugstore. The room was near the stairs leading down to the drugstore's basement. Officials later said there may have been a gas leak from a pipe in the basement. They speculated that the gas had collected in the basement, where it built up unnoticed and slowly rose up the stairway. The two young men were mixing chemicals used to develop photographs. There was a small gas lamp with an open flame in the darkroom. The lamp went out, and when Emsley Johnson lit a match to relight the lamp, an explosion occurred.

Edgar Watts later testified at the coroner's inquest that none of the chemicals he used in the darkroom were explosive. This testimony was in response to the gas company's claim that the explosion was caused by chemicals in stock at the drugstore rather than a gas explosion. Watts said that Johnson lit a match, and the atmosphere inside the darkroom suddenly turned bright green as everything exploded. Both men were knocked down and dazed but made it out of the building. Later, neither could recall exactly how they'd escaped. Both men were burned, with Edgar suffering severe injuries. The other men, who'd been inside the drugstore, managed to free themselves. They had injuries ranging from broken bones to burns, but none were life-threatening.

Squire Culbertson and his son Charles were sitting in their wagon. They happened to be parked in front of the drugstore when the explosion occurred. They were struck by flying debris and window glass but were not seriously injured. However, their horse was startled by the noise and concussion of the blast. It bolted and caused the wagon to overturn, throwing the two men into the street.

The explosion shook the entire town of Broad Ripple, with the concussion felt over a wide area. The September 4, 1897 *Indianapolis News* reported that farmers two miles north of Broad Ripple heard the blast. They rushed to town to find out what had happened. The explosion broke a lot of windows in the small town. The blast reduced the drugstore to rubble, and the remains caught fire almost immediately.

At that time, Broad Ripple was protected by a volunteer fire department. In 1897, the town purchased a hand pumper, three hundred feet of hose and a twenty-gallon chemical fire extinguisher for their small department. The volunteers responded promptly to this incident. However, they encountered problems when they couldn't find a water source near the fire. Broad Ripple had no hydrants or cisterns for firefighting. Not finding a nearby well, firefighters tried laying a hose line to the White River to establish a water supply. However, they didn't have enough hose to reach the river. The volunteers finally abandoned their efforts with their hand pumper and formed a bucket brigade. Many local citizens helped in this endeavor. Unfortunately, it wasn't very effective against the raging flames they were facing.

The fire soon threatened the building east of the drugstore. That two-story frame structure was known as the Odd Fellows building. It housed Gresh's Grocery Store on the ground floor and the Independent Order of Odd Fellows, a fraternal club, on its second floor. It was located on the west side of Airline Street (now Cornell Avenue) north of Main Street.

The limited firefighting resources soon made it apparent that the Odd Fellows building would succumb to the flames. Bystanders rushed into the grocery and began bringing out whatever they could salvage before the fire consumed the building. About a dozen men were working inside the burning store when another large explosion occurred. This one destroyed the Odd Fellows building, with natural gas again suspected as the cause. All four walls were pushed outward, and the roof and second floor collapsed into the structure, trapping several men in the wreckage. The building was destroyed.

Immediately, shocked bystanders began rescue efforts to help the trapped men. These weren't just nameless victims; they were neighbors and friends trapped in the wreckage.

An official at Broad Ripple's Monon train station telephoned Indianapolis at about 10:30 a.m., asking for help for his community. He requested the fire department, doctors and police. Unfortunately, the official had a front-row seat for the fire, since it was happening directly across the street from his railroad station.

An ambulance and five doctors started to the scene from City Hospital. In addition, the Indianapolis Police Department sent a squad of officers.

The Indianapolis Fire Department sent Chief Thomas Barrett, an engine and a hose wagon to the Monon Railroad Freight Depot at New Jersey and Pearl Streets. Upon arriving there, they were supposed to board a special train that would take them to Broad Ripple. They sent these companies by train from the downtown area because, in 1897, only three Indianapolis firehouses were further north than Sixteenth Street. They were Station no. 9 at Udell (2850 North) Street and Rader Streets, Station no. 14 at Thirtieth (3000 North) Street and Kenwood Avenue and Station no. 16 at Sixteenth (1600 North) Street and Carrolton Avenue. Only Station no. 9 had a pumper. The other two stations were hose companies. Rather than leave the north side partially unprotected, the fire department sent a pumper and hose wagon from one of the downtown stations, where more fire companies were available.

(A note about Indianapolis addresses: they are calculated from the downtown intersection of Washington and Meridian Streets, so 1600 North is 1.6 miles north of Washington Street, 3000 North is 3 miles north, et cetera. The fire in Broad Ripple was at about 6300 North, or 6.3 miles north of Washington Street.)

By sending the fire apparatus by train, it set in motion what could only be called a tragic "comedy of errors." When the fire department arrived at the railroad depot, they were told they weren't needed. The telephone operator at the depot informed the chief that he'd received a message saying the fire was out. The chief and the fire apparatus returned to their stations. It was never learned where this message originated, but it was wrong—very wrong.

Over an hour later, the fires were still burning out of control, and everyone in Broad Ripple wondered where the Indianapolis Fire Department was. Captain James Quigley, an Indianapolis police officer in Broad Ripple, finally called the fire alarm office. He told the alarm operator how desperately Broad Ripple needed help from the fire department. So, once again, the chief and the other fire companies were sent to the freight depot to board the train.

However, they couldn't leave yet. That was because the crew of the special train, which was supposed to take them to Broad Ripple, had to finish their union-mandated lunch hour before they started the trip. So, despite the emergency, the train couldn't move until the crew completed their lunch hour.

Meanwhile, rescue efforts continued in the shattered town. A few men trapped in Gresh's Grocery escaped the wreckage by themselves. Several of them needed assistance, while others were beyond all help. As rescuers swarmed the ruins, the first victim found was Jacob "Jack" Darling, age fifty-five. He died when he was crushed by a falling wall. His body was removed from the wreckage before the flames got to it.

Clare Whittaker was extricated with difficulty. He was pinned by several heavy boards that had to be cut away. He was carried out with bruises and a broken ankle. Orval Heady was rescued after suffering from internal injuries and burns on his head and face.

Other victims were not so lucky. The wreckage of the store was burning out of control. Reluctantly, rescuers had to abandon their efforts due to the approaching flames. Some of the trapped men had died before the fire reached them. Unfortunately, others were still alive as the flames approached.

Several men had been working to rescue Pius Gresh, the nineteen-year-old son of the grocery owner. He was in the remains with three or four large timbers pinning his legs and another lying across his chest. These timbers were too heavy to lift off Gresh, so rescuers were frantically chopping and sawing through them, trying to free him. That was a time-consuming process. As the flames drew closer, rescuers were finally forced to abandon Pius Gresh to his horrible fate. The rescuers and the other spectators had to endure hearing the agonized screams of young Gresh for several minutes before the flames silenced him forever. Nearby, onlookers heard another voice pleading for help, but the flames and heat also prevented his rescue.

That victim was Charles Yount, a local resident, age thirty-five, who had no connection with the grocery other than the fact that he was a good neighbor. Rescue workers had tried valiantly but couldn't free him in time. He had selflessly volunteered to help salvage the grocery's merchandise. Unfortunately, it cost him his life.

Suddenly, while the wreckage was burning out of control, some movement was noticed in the debris. As the crowd looked on in horror, a victim was seen struggling to escape the rubble. Sadly, no one could assist him due to the intense heat. Finally, after working for several minutes, Edward Morris was able to free himself and escape the blaze. He managed this despite a broken right arm. He also suffered flame inhalation and severe burns to his face, right arm and hands, but he eventually recovered from his injuries.

Although Thomas Mitchell was seventy-one years old, he was another of the men who was helping to salvage items from the grocery store. He was injured when a wall fell on him. That caused a compound fracture in his left leg and spinal injuries. His family learned of his injuries, and they rushed to Broad Ripple. Despite protests from doctors, his family insisted on returning him to his home in New Augusta about fourteen miles away. After his were injuries tended to, his family was allowed to take him home in a buggy. Due to his age and the injuries, doctors were concerned that he wouldn't survive the trip. He made it home, only to die there a few hours later.

Albert Haworth, a forty-two-year-old farmer, lived near Westfield. He'd come to town on that fateful morning to buy provisions. Leaving his horse and wagon hitched to a post, Haworth went into a local hardware store. Finished with his shopping, he was putting supplies in the wagon when the first explosion occurred. After quickly running to the scene, he began helping the injured men from the drugstore. Seeing that the fire threatened the grocery store, he immediately began helping remove its stock. Unfortunately, Mr. Haworth was inside the grocery when the second explosion occurred. His body was later recovered, burned beyond recognition.

John Porter, age eighteen, lived on a farm a few miles north of Broad Ripple. Like the other victims, he had been helping in the grocery salvage efforts when he died. His remains, badly burned, were recovered later in the day.

Henry Ernst was a sixty-five-year-old Civil War veteran who worked at a local hotel and lived in Broad Ripple. Like the other victims, Mr. Ernst had unselfishly gone into the grocery to help his neighbors and also paid with his life.

Over two dozen people were injured in the explosions and while attempting to free the trapped men. Their injuries ranged from cuts and bruises to broken bones, burns and internal injuries. A local hotel called the Hoffman House was turned into a makeshift hospital. Local doctors, along with the doctors from Indianapolis, treated the injured. Some of the victims with serious injuries were transported to City Hospital in Indianapolis for further treatment.

The damage wasn't confined to just the two buildings damaged by the explosions. The entire block, bounded by Main Street to the south, Cherry Street (now Guilford Avenue) to the west, North Street (now Sixty-Fourth Street) to the north and Airline Street (now Cornell Avenue) to the east, was devastated. Besides Watt's Drugstore building and the Odd Fellows and Gresh's Grocery building, a house and barn owned by Manford Lange was destroyed by the fire, along with White's Livery Stable. Those four streets served as fire breaks, so the blaze did not spread beyond these boundaries despite a lack of effective firefighting. No animals died in either the stable or the barn fires.

The chief and two companies from the Indianapolis Fire Department, delayed through no fault of their own, finally made it to the scene at about 1:30 p.m. By then, most of the fires had burned themselves out, and the danger of the fire spreading was over. The pumper drafted from the White River, and its hose lines were used to cool the ruins so the victim's bodies could be removed.

The Marion County coroner, Alembert Brayton, held an inquest into the incident. Gas company officials testified that they believed natural gas had not caused the explosions. Instead, they insisted that the explosions were caused by the various chemicals, flammable liquids and gunpowder present in the stock of both businesses.

However, the coroner determined that the explosions were caused by leaking natural gas in both buildings. The service lines that supplied gas to the drugstore and the grocery store were dug up and examined as part of the investigation. Several small holes, possibly caused by corrosion, were found in both pipes. The coroner also noted that the gas company had not installed these service lines running from the gas main to the buildings. Instead, the owners of both structures had been allowed to install these service lines themselves.

The coroner did not put place the blame for the gas leak on the gas company. He also failed to blame the store owners, who had installed the service lines from the gas company's main supply line to their businesses.

Instead, Coroner Brayton simply gave the cause for the deaths as explosions and fires caused by leaking natural gas without directly blaming anyone for the leaks.

Coroner Brayton ruled that two victims, Thomas Mitchell and Jacob Darling, died due to injuries caused by the explosion and subsequent collapse of the Odd Fellows building. The bodies of the other five victims were so badly burned that the coroner could not determine whether they'd been killed by their injuries before the fire or from their burns. Therefore, he ruled that each of the five had burned to death.

In addition to the seven deaths and many injuries, the loss of Watts' Drug Store building and contents was $3,300 ($118,486); the Odd Fellows Building and contents, including Gresh's Grocery, was $3,500 ($125,667); Manford Lange's home and barn loss was $800 ($28,724); and White's Livery Stable was $1,000 ($35,905).

Today, a modern three-story apartment building occupies the block where several buildings were destroyed and seven people died.

10

THE C.B. CONES AND SON OVERALL FACTORY FIRE

C.B. Cones and Son began manufacturing clothing in 1879, making overalls for workers and farmers. It started in a small facility with only six sewing machines and about a dozen employees, and it sold most of its garments locally. Then in less than ten years, the company grew to be the largest manufacturer of overalls in the world. It now occupied four floors of a building on South Meridian Street and three more in another building next door.

At least it did until Friday, January 13, 1888. Late that evening, a fire was discovered in a building on the east side of Meridian Street, just south of Georgia Street. By the time the blaze was brought under control, it had destroyed or damaged fifteen buildings on both sides of South Meridian Street, resulting in a loss of $770,000 ($24,154,495). The two buildings that were home to C.B. Cones and Sons were among the nine structures lost.

After this devastating fire, Cones needed a new location to continue its business. It had many clothing orders and needed to fill them quickly. It soon secured temporary quarters while looking for a more permanent site for its factory. Since time was a factor, the owners decided to renovate an existing building rather than take the time to build a new structure.

They found what they wanted on the south side of Court Street, west of Senate Avenue. This location was just west of the Indiana State House and a half block north of Washington Street. Two separate buildings were located there that were constructed end to end, with a common wall between them.

Both buildings had interesting histories. The western structure had previously been a theater. It had a large stage at its west end. On the east side was a building that was once an exposition hall that housed an indoor zoo. The zoo had gone out of business several years before. Since then, the building had been used for various displays and exhibitions before it was purchased by Cones.

Together, the two buildings measured about forty-five by two hundred feet. Both of them were wood-frame and about forty feet tall. The eastern structure had a brick veneer, and the west building had wood siding. The brick veneer on the east building was retained, while the wood siding on the western portion was covered by sheets of iron nailed to the siding. The iron sheets were an attempt to make the wood siding more fire resistant.

Contractors gutted the two buildings and tore down the shared wall between them. They then added two floors inside the spacious structure. So, now there was one large factory building with three floors inside. They held various cloth-cutting, sewing and other types of machinery, along with offices.

Within a short time, the new C.B. Cones and Son Company factory was operating at full capacity, turning out over four thousand garments daily. It had a workforce of over four hundred people, a majority of whom were women.

The new facility was not without its problems, however. Both structures were already old when they were rebuilt to become Cones's new factory. Despite these renovations, the structures remained in a somewhat dilapidated condition.

John Robinson, the Indianapolis building inspector, had attempted to condemn the Cones building several times. In each case, someone reported that a part of the building was in poor condition or close to collapsing. After an inspection, the city would begin efforts to condemn the building. That process could take a while. At that point, Cones would hire workers to do whatever was necessary to bring the building back into compliance with the law. Then the city would be forced to halt the condemnation proceedings. Cones and the building inspector went back and forth like this several times.

Inspector Robinson grew frustrated with these manipulations of the law, saying, "There is no law by which we can condemn a fire trap unless it is in danger of falling down. Then, if it is propped up enough to make it stand safely, nothing more can be done about it!"

Given that the building was old and in relatively poor shape, it was fortunate that this fire occurred in the evening, after the garment workers had left for the day. Otherwise, the flames' rapid spread could have endangered the lives of hundreds of employees.

On the evening of Wednesday, March 14, 1900, two workmen were installing a new gas burner in the engine room. Arthur Smith and Sam Watters, the two installers, had been working for a couple of hours when, at about 9:00 p.m., they found that they needed additional tools from their nearby workshop. Watters had left the building, and Smith was just leaving. As he opened the rear door, a large explosion occurred. Officials later speculated that a gas line had been leaking for a while and then found an ignition source. Smith was blown ten feet into the alley but was uninjured.

Emanuel Hoefgen, the building's night watchman, was making his rounds on the third floor at the time. When he heard the explosion, he hurried down to the first floor. He saw the entire west end of the factory heavily involved in fire. He called the fire department from the factory's business office and quickly fled the building. At about the same time, Sam Watters ran to the corner of Senate Avenue and Washington Street and sent an alarm from box no. 417. The alarm office dispatched the first alarm at 9:04 p.m.

The first arriving units found the wood-framed C.B. Cones and Son Company already heavily involved with a rapidly spreading fire. Chief Thomas Barrett was on the scene within four minutes of the initial alarm and immediately sent in a second alarm. Seven minutes after the second alarm, he called for a third alarm, which brought much of the fire department to the scene.

One of the first companies to arrive was Engine no. 1. They quickly had a hose line working on the northwest portion of the building, where the initial explosion had occurred. Unfortunately, as they fought the flames, a large portion of the north wall collapsed. That sent heavy framing timbers, roofing material, wood siding and iron sheets that had been nailed to the siding raining down on the crew. Four firefighters, Frank Mankin, Patrick McMahan, Orlando Wesby and Ed Hartnett, were trapped beneath a large pile of flaming debris. Luckily, Sergeant John Lowe, a policeman, saw what had happened. Not seeing any other firefighters nearby, he called two other police officers to assist him. Detective William Holtz and Sergeant Harry Wallace helped in the rescue.

Several people from the crowd of spectators also assisted with the rescue. At first, the police officers attempted to use the firefighters' hose to extinguish the debris. Engine no. 1's crew dropped the hose as the collapse occurred, and it hadn't been trapped in the rubble with them. Not being used to the hose's high pressure, the officers couldn't control it and use it as they intended.

They gave up on the hose, and the police officers and spectators began using their bare hands to pull the debris off the trapped men. After the rescuers had removed enough wreckage, three of the firefighters were able to extricate themselves. These firefighters had minor burns and bruises but were otherwise uninjured. The fourth firefighter, Frank Mankin, was finally pulled free, but his legs had been badly burned. An ambulance rushed Mankin to City Hospital for treatment. The rest of Frank Mankin's story is told later in this chapter.

This author found accounts of this fire in the *Indianapolis Journal*, *Indianapolis Sun* and *Indianapolis News*. However, the *Journal*'s and the *Sun*'s articles only credited the policemen and some spectators with the rescue.

On the other hand, the *Indianapolis News* reported, "The members of the No. 10 Hose Company, who were working nearby, ran to the assistance of the imprisoned men." The article continued, "The crowd standing in Court Street surged forward with the police, and several of them rendered assistance in tearing away the debris which held the imprisoned men. Conspicuous among the rescuers was Tony O'Hara, who was slightly burned about the hands." That was the only newspaper account that mentioned any fire department members having a role in rescuing Engine no. 1's trapped men.

After the firefighters were freed, someone thought they heard moaning from the debris pile. At about the same time, bystanders noticed Captain Jim George of Engine no. 1, well known to citizens in the area, didn't seem to be with his crew. Was he trapped under the debris? Luckily, they quickly learned Captain George wasn't on duty that day. The debris pile was searched again, but fortunately, no other victims were found.

The fire spread so quickly that, within a short time, Chief Barrett ordered firefighters to abandon their fight to save the Cones building. Instead, he told them to concentrate their efforts on the exposures. The main concern was a row of brick buildings built side by side that fronted Washington Street, immediately south of the Cones building. Only a fifteen-foot-wide alley, oriented east–west, separated the blazing Cones building and the rear of these structures. Unfortunately, nature was also working against the firefighting efforts. A brisk wind was blowing directly south, sending flames, heat and sparks into the rear of these buildings.

The row of buildings all had West Washington Street addresses. Beginning at the northwest corner of Washington Street and Senate Avenue and proceeding west, the addresses and occupancies were as follows: 302, an eighteen-by-seventy-five-foot, two-story brick saloon; 304, a seventeen-by-seventy-five-foot, two-story brick saloon; 306, an eighteen-by-sixty-foot, two-story brick clothing store; 310, a seventeen-by-sixty-foot, two-story brick tea store; 312, an eighteen-by-sixty-foot, two-story brick liquor store; 316, an eighteen-by-seventy-five-foot, two-story brick shoe store; and 320, a twenty-by-seventy-five-foot, three-story, brick drugstore. The next building was a thirty-eight-by-sixty-five-foot, three-story brick structure with two occupancies: 322, a clothing store; and 326, a liquor store. There was a twenty-by-ten-foot, one-story brick addition in the rear of the liquor store. The last building in this row was a thirty-eight-by-fifty-foot, two-story brick structure. It also had two tenants: 330, a dry goods store; and 334, a saloon. There was a ten-by-twenty-five-foot, one-story, wood-framed addition in the rear of the dry goods store. All of these structures were in danger from the wind-driven flames coming from the Cones building.

The various stores and saloons were located on the first floors of the buildings, while the upper floors of most of the buildings contained apartments. The exceptions were the two floors above the drugstore at 320 West Washington Street. The March 15, 1900 edition of the *Indianapolis Journal* reported that those floors were occupied by a "resort" (a euphemism for a brothel) run by a woman named Lillie Darrow. The same article also mentioned that after Frank Mankin was injured, he was carried into a nearby house on Court Street. The newspaper said that the dwelling was also a "resort." A doctor was called to treat Mankin while he waited for the ambulance.

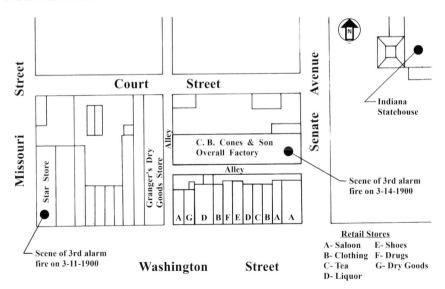

A map showing the area of the C.B. Cones and Son fire. Flames and smoke threatened the row of retail stores and the Granger Store. *Map by author.*

An apartment above the tea store was the scene of a dramatic rescue. John King and his wife had lived in the apartment for many years. Both of them were elderly and had severe arthritis, making it very difficult for them to walk. The regular access to their apartment was a stairway at the rear of the building. Unfortunately, this stairway could not be reached due to the heavy flames and heat from the fire across the alley. As a result, the incapacitated couple was trapped in their apartment. Luckily, John Breen, a policeman who regularly patrolled this area, was familiar with the Kings' infirmities and the difficulty in gaining access to their apartment due to the fire. Breen found a ladder and raised it to the couple's apartment window on the Washington Street side. He climbed into the apartment and carried Mrs. King down the ladder to a safe place. He then returned and carried Mr. King to safety. Neither of the Kings suffered any injuries.

Directly west of the row of buildings on Washington Street and the Cones building was a fifteen-foot-wide alley called Osage Street, which ran north–south. On the west side of Osage was the 32-by-250 foot, two-story brick Granger Dry Goods Store, which fronted on Washington Street and extended north, back to Court Street. It had an address of 336 and 338 West Washington Street. Unfortunately, the western wall of the Cones building had collapsed into Osage Street, exposing the Granger building to high heat and flames. Despite this, firefighters kept the fire from damaging this department store, although its stock suffered about $3,000 ($106,432) in smoke damage.

The fire department's water tower responded with the second alarm. That specialized apparatus was positioned so that its stream and streams from several Glazier nozzles were directed into the narrow alley south of the Coles building. That provided a water curtain to protect the rear of the buildings on Washington Street. The water did have the desired effect of keeping most of the flames out of these structures. The buildings themselves did suffer some damage, reported to be about $20,000 ($709,548) total. However, all of that water had to go somewhere. Most of it flooded the basements of the row of buildings. These eleven establishments had total combined damages to their merchandise of about $31,000 ($1,099,799). Much of this accounted for the merchandise ruined when the basements flooded.

It was later alleged that one store owner had intentionally damaged his own shop. A couple of weeks after the fire, two employees of the liquor store at 312 West Washington Street accused the store owner of arson. They claimed that Isaac Nier had deliberately set a fire in the store and then collected $900 ($31,930) from his insurance company. The two clerks said that on the night of the Cones fire, soon after the initial alarm, they saw Nier set fire to some boxes in the rear of the store.

Chief Thomas Barrett had investigated the fire in the liquor store and was puzzled about how the Cones fire could have caused the fire in the liquor store. However, he found no evidence that the liquor store fire had been deliberately set.

Isaac Nier initially offered the two employees $150 ($5,322) each if they would keep quiet about what they'd seen that night. Later though, he refused to pay them, and they went to the police. As a result, Isaac Nier was arrested on arson charges. However, on June 18, 1900, a grand jury decided there was insufficient evidence to charge him with arson.

C.B. Cones and Son sustained the largest amount of damage. Their building was almost destroyed, with only a few brick walls remaining. It also lost everything inside its building. About three hundred sewing machines, other pieces of machinery, office equipment, completed clothing and large quantities of materials for clothing manufacturing were badly damaged or destroyed. The damage estimate to the building and contents was $140,000 ($4,966,833).

Amazingly, the Cones fire was not the only large fire in this block during the same week. On Sunday evening, just three days before the Cones fire, another fire caused an estimated $120,000 ($4,257,286) in damages to the building and merchandise of the Star Department Store. The Star Store was a 50-by-250-foot, four-story brick building located at 360–370 West Washington Street. It stood on the northeast corner of Washington and Missouri Streets, just half a block west of the row of buildings threatened by the Cones fire. The Star Store fire also required a third alarm response before it was brought under control. This fire caused no injuries. Its origin was thought to have been an overheated furnace in the basement.

Frank Mankin, the firefighter injured when the wall collapsed during the Cones fire, was born in Hancock County, Indiana, on February 25, 1869. He joined the fire department on December 16, 1899, and was assigned to Hose Company no. 15. Two months later, he was sent to Hose Company no. 1, located on Indiana Avenue, south of Michigan Street. He was working in this company when he was injured. An ambulance took him to City Hospital, where initial reports on his injury were encouraging. Chief Barrett visited him the next morning and reported that his injury was not serious. A few days later, the *Indianapolis Sun* said, "His injuries are not serious, but will keep him confined in the hospital for several days." On March 26, the same newspaper reported, "Frank Mankin will have a stiff leg for some time,

Station no. 6 was located at 533 West Washington Street from 1875 until 1935. This firehouse responded to the Cones fire and several other incidents mentioned in this book. This photograph is from early 1900s. *The Indianapolis Firefighters Museum.*

but the doctors say it will eventually be well." By April 5, the *Indianapolis News* was reporting, "Frank Mankin is still in the hospital. His leg is burned to the bone, and it is feared that his injuries may be permanent." On April 16, it was reported that Mankin was in critical condition. The next day, in an attempt to save his life, doctors amputated his left leg at the mid-thigh. Unfortunately, at 4:00 a.m., on April 19, 1900, Frank Elmer Mankin died from his injuries.

His funeral was held on April 22 at the home of his sister, Maude, who lived at 412 North Delaware Street. His only other surviving family member was his father, A.J. Mankin of Watseka, Illinois. The pallbearers were all members of Engine no. 1 and included the other three firefighters who had been caught in the collapse with Mankin. After the funeral, the pallbearers accompanied his family to the burial service. He was laid to rest in Simmon's Cemetery in Hancock County, Indiana. That was the same cemetery where his mother was buried after her death in 1894.

Today, the State of Indiana's Government Center South building covers the site where the C.B. Cones and Son overall factory once stood. In addition, the location of the buildings threatened during the Cones fire and the one damaged in the Star Store fire, along with Missouri Street itself, are now covered by that same government building.

A small plaza is located just a few hundred feet north of where Cones factory once stood. The plaza is on the east side of the Indiana Government Center North building and is home to the Indiana Law Enforcement and Firefighters Memorial. This memorial is dedicated to all the firefighters and law enforcement officers from across Indiana who have died in the line of duty. Frank E. Mankin is among the many honored there.

11

THE PURDUE TRAIN WRECK

In late October 1903, many people in Indiana were excited about an upcoming football game. Longtime rivals Purdue University, located in West Lafayette, Indiana, and Indiana University in Bloomington, Indiana, were to meet on Halloween afternoon, October 31, 1903. They would be playing at Washington Park in Indianapolis. That was a minor league baseball park located on the southwest corner of East Washington and Gray Streets. The American Association's Indianapolis Indians baseball team called this ballpark home from 1902 to 1904.

Indianapolis was chosen because, in the past, there had been problems when games were played at the schools. Sometimes, hometown fans were overzealous and caused trouble for the opposing school. By playing in "neutral territory," the schools hoped to squelch any unruly behavior, since neither team would be the "home" team.

There would be a large audience at this football game. Purdue students had bought one thousand tickets and telegraphed an order for four hundred more. Indiana University students purchased a similar amount. With alumni from both schools and many other fans clamoring for tickets, it promised to be the largest crowd ever to witness a football game in Indiana.

In those days, before automobiles were commonplace, schools often chartered trains to take players and fans to away games. Purdue was no exception. It had enough students and fans making the trip to need two trains to accommodate everyone. It chartered these trains from the Cleveland, Cincinnati, Chicago and St. Louis Railroad Company, commonly known as the "Big Four" railroad.

The first train consisted of a steam engine, tender and fourteen passenger cars filled with over nine hundred enthusiastic students. That train left the station in Lafayette at 8:00 a.m. and was due at Union Station in Indianapolis at 9:47 a.m. The second Purdue train left fifteen minutes after the first one. The Big Four Railroad had designated the two trains as "specials." This meant that both Purdue trains were supposed to have priority over every other train using the track. Therefore, any train on the main railroad track from Lafayette to Indianapolis between 8:00 a.m. and 9:47 a.m. would be required to pull onto a side track until both Purdue specials had passed. Their "special" status also meant that the two trains could travel as fast as they felt was safe and necessary.

Despite this, the first train was running about ten minutes behind schedule when it reached the outskirts of Indianapolis. According to railroad rules, the engineer was supposed to slow the train when it arrived at North Indianapolis, where the Big Four railroad and the Indianapolis Belt Line Railroad intersected. He was then supposed to keep the speed slow enough to, as the rule read, "fully stop the train before it encountered any obstruction." This rule was supposed to be applied under any circumstance, such as ice on the tracks, fog, rain, curves that made it difficult to see very far ahead, et cetera. The engineer was expected to "keep the train under control and be able to stop it within a reasonable distance."

The engineer on the first Purdue train later testified that he was running his train at eighteen to twenty miles per hour at the time of the accident. However, many witnesses, both passengers on the train and bystanders who saw the accident, testified that they estimated the train's speed to be as high as forty miles per hour.

At the same time that the Purdue specials were traveling toward the north side of Indianapolis, another train crew was delivering coal to commercial and industrial customers in Indianapolis. Engineer Edward Smith and fireman John Clemens were running a train consisting of a switch engine and seven coal cars, each weighing forty tons. Unfortunately, their dispatcher never informed them of the two Purdue trains speeding toward Union Station. Just before 10:00 a.m., the coal train was moving north at about nine miles per hour on the main track. The coal train was backing up on the tracks, meaning the engine was at the south end of the train, pushing the string of coal cars north. Because of this, the train's crew did not have a clear view of where they were going, since they had to look across the seven coal cars to see ahead.

Meanwhile, the two Purdue specials were southbound, unaware they were not alone on the main track. Then as the first Purdue train rounded a broad curve just north of Eighteenth Street and east of Mill Street, it also encountered problems with seeing ahead. That was because the railroad had parked empty coal cars on a siding west of the main track, blocking the train's view toward the south. So, as the first train rounded the curve, the crew suddenly saw, to their horror, a line of coal cars occupying the same track they were on.

Reacting quickly, the Purdue train's engineer, William Schumaker, applied the brakes and threw his engine into reverse, desperately trying to slow it down. He then jumped from the train, hoping to avoid injury. The train's fireman, A.B. Irvan, climbed onto the coal piled in the tender behind the engine to try to ride out the wreck. Despite the engineer's efforts to slow the train, the Purdue engine hit the first coal car with a deafening roar. The engine derailed and fell on its side, pulling the tender over with it. Still moving forward, it collided with one of the coal cars parked on the siding. The fireman riding atop the tender was buried as coal spilled from the overturned car. He dug himself out, suffering only minor bruising. None of the Purdue train crew were seriously injured. The coal train crew at the opposite end of the collision were uninjured.

The passenger car immediately behind the tender held the Purdue football team, their coaches and trainers and some fans. That car suffered the most damage. The train's momentum forcibly carried it into the wreckage of the locomotive, its tender and the coal cars. As it hit, it split from end to end, reared up into the air and fell back, breaking into pieces. Those who heard the crash could never forget the sound—wood breaking, glass shattering, metal grinding, people screaming. It was horrendous. Most of its passengers were ejected. Several victims were crushed beneath the locomotive and its tender. The only recognizable parts of the car were part of the roof and a portion of one side.

The second passenger car contained the Purdue band. The car rode up and over the coal cars, falling on its side and partly sliding down a fifteen-foot embankment on the east side of the main track. It stopped with one end next to the tracks and the other at the bottom of the fifteen-foot embankment. All its passengers wound up in a tangled heap at the lower end of the car.

The third car also rode up and onto one of the coal cars. It came to rest there, perched on top of the other car like toys some gigantic child had stacked together. The fourth passenger car derailed but stayed upright alongside the track. The rest of the train's cars remained on track. In fact, passengers in railroad cars toward the rear were not even aware that there had been an accident. All they felt was a sudden jolt, which threw some of

RELIEF WORK AT THE WRECK.

An illustration from the *Indianapolis Star* showing victims of the Purdue railroad wreck being tended to. *Courtesy of the Indianapolis Star.*

them against the seat in front of them as the train quickly stopped. It wasn't until they got off the train to find out why it had stopped that they learned of the awful carnage at the front of the train.

Quick thinking helped to prevent a second accident. Knowing the other Purdue train was approaching the accident scene, a man with a warning flag ran back to halt it. He managed to warn the train in time and kept it from crashing into the back of the stopped train. The second train started fifteen minutes behind the first but was able to make better speed. At the time of the accident, it was only five minutes behind the first train.

All of the dead and many injured victims were occupants of the first car. A total of seventeen victims, all men, died. Twelve were killed on impact, while five more died after being taken to area hospitals. Three victims died later that same day. One of the victims died the following day, while the seventeenth victim suffered for almost a month before dying on November 30, 1903.

Fourteen of the victims were Purdue students. The other three were adults: one was a trainer, one was an assistant coach and one was a team fan. In a bit of irony, the accident happened on the 101st anniversary of the birth of Purdue's benefactor, John Purdue.

Besides the deaths, there were many injuries, with more than forty victims who required hospitalization. Several remained in area hospitals for months.

Initially, the injured were taken to hospitals by whatever vehicles were nearby. Then ambulances began arriving from various hospitals. Finally, when that still wasn't enough to transport all the injured victims, fire department hose wagons and even hearses carried the victims.

View of the Passenger Coaches After the Smash-up.

An illustration from the *Indianapolis Journal* showing the wreck site. One coach is sitting on top of a coal car. One is lying tilted on the embankment. Some of the remains of the first coach are also visible. *Courtesy of the* Indianapolis Journal.

The injured victims were taken to several Indianapolis hospitals. Deaconess Hospital, City Hospital and St. Vincent's Hospital received patients from the accident. Unfortunately, Methodist Hospital, which would have been very close to the accident scene, would not open for another four and a half years.

Besides these hospitals, Dr. Samuel Cunningham, who lived less than a block from the accident scene, turned his home into a hospital and treated victims. Some remained there, under his care, for several weeks.

When news of the wreck reached the Medical College of Indiana, the school immediately sent all senior class members to various hospitals to render whatever assistance they could. Frank Truitt and some of his classmates reported to City Hospital. While he was there, two ambulance attendants brought in a victim on a stretcher. "Doctor, this man looks like he's dead," said one of the attendants. As Truitt bent down to examine the victim, he recognized his own brother, Samuel. Unfortunately, the attendant was correct, and Frank Truitt pronounced his brother dead.

The noise of the accident echoed through neighborhoods around the scene, causing many people to rush to the incident. Many who had witnessed the crash brought bandages, drinking water, towels and other supplies to help the injured victims.

After the injured victims had all been cared for, recovery of the dead began. Unfortunately, several bodies were under the tender and the locomotive. Railroad crews, police and firefighters used heavy-duty jacks to lift these massive vehicles and remove the bodies.

The railroad crews brought in cranes to clear away the wreckage. Crews worked so efficiently that they had the debris cleared away and the railroad tracks repaired by 6:00 p.m. Just eight hours after the accident, trains were again using the tracks.

Among the dozens of injured students was future political standout Harry G. Leslie. He would, twenty-six years later, be elected governor of Indiana. He'd been riding in the first coach with the rest of the football team. Mr. Leslie had played football throughout his college career and had been the captain of the team in 1902. He also played baseball for the school and was captain of that team. In addition, he was the president of the class of 1904.

Initially, newspapers reported that Harry Leslie had died in the crash. Then they said that he was hospitalized but could not survive his injuries. Despite these dire predictions, he did survive. He suffered a broken jaw, a severely broken leg, a concussion and internal injuries. He remained in the hospital for over two months and endured several operations. Then after being released from the hospital, he reinjured his leg and had to have it operated on again. While recuperating from that operation, he came down with typhoid fever and almost died from that. Eventually, he was able to return to Purdue. However, due to all the classes he'd missed during his hospitalization, he couldn't graduate until 1905. He went on to attend law school and begin a career as a lawyer. Sometime later, he became involved in politics and, after serving in several capacities within the state government, was elected governor of Indiana in 1929. He served one term and then left politics to serve as president of an insurance company.

When news of the catastrophe reached Lafayette and West Lafayette, the home of Purdue, people rushed from their homes and businesses to gather in downtown Lafayette to learn the latest news of the wreck. Some area citizens had sons and daughters who attended Purdue and were known to be on the train. They crowded into telegraph, telephone and newspaper offices, seeking news of their loved ones.

At 1:37 p.m., a train coming from Indianapolis reached Lafayette. It held many students who had survived the wreck. Other students onboard had been on the second "special," which was not involved in the accident. However, all of the students were shocked and grief-stricken. Three thousand people were on hand to meet this train.

The Indiana University football team and its supporters had also taken a train to Indianapolis. With the team and over one thousand students and fans, that train approached Indianapolis from the school's southern Indiana hometown of Bloomington. Everyone onboard was chanting and cheering for IU during the trip. It wasn't until they disembarked at the Indianapolis Union Station that they learned of the terrible accident that had befallen their rivals. The fans, many of whom were wearing ribbons with their school's colors of cream and crimson, quickly put these bright ribbons away and purchased black ribbons to signify mourning.

IU's President, Dr. William Bryan, who'd been on the train, obtained an automobile and drove to the accident scene to offer his and his school's help. He later met his counterpart, Purdue President Winthrop Stone, at Indianapolis's Denison House Hotel to help arrange the care for all the injured persons.

Meanwhile, there were rumors that the Indiana University train had met with minor misfortune while on its trip. People were saying that one car of the IU train had briefly come off the tracks but corrected itself before any wreck could occur. There were other rumors that some of the train's crew had a premonition of a disaster involving the IU train. Allegedly, some crew members refused to work on the train because of these omens. Finally, a crew unconcerned by any talk of premonitions was assembled to work on the train. After an investigation, railroad officials could find no basis for either of these rumors.

Mr. and Mrs. William Roush from Gas City, Indiana, had the awful experience of learning of their son Walter's death from a newspaper. They had been visiting friends in Anderson, Indiana, and were getting ready to board a train to attend the big football game in Indianapolis when Mrs. Roush heard newsboys shouting, "Extra! Extra! Read all about the big Purdue train wreck!" Worried about her son, who she knew was on the train, she bought a paper, and upon reading Walter's name in the list of fatalities, she fainted. Her husband, who was deaf, couldn't understand why she'd passed out. Finally, someone handed him the newspaper, and he read the awful news himself.

At least one of the survivors wasn't human. Thousand Dollars was the unofficial mascot for the football team. He was a Scotch collie dog whose natural coloring happened to be Purdue's black and gold. He also had some white in his fur. He'd attended every Purdue game that year, so of course, he was on the train, riding in the second car with the band. He was later found wandering, uninjured, among the wreckage. Arthur Hoffman, a Purdue student, recognized the mascot. He took him to the home of Fred Riebel, another Purdue student who lived in Indianapolis. The dog's owner, Harry Leslie, was severely injured and hospitalized for several months. Riebel and his family cared for the mascot until Mr. Leslie was released and could care for Thousand Dollars again.

On Sunday afternoon, the day after the wreck, Cleveland, Cincinnati, Chicago and St. Louis Railroad officials blamed the accident on the crew of the first Purdue special. They reasoned that the crew could have prevented the accident if they'd kept the train under proper control, as the rules required. However, their ruling would have no bearing on the coroner's inquest.

The Marion County coroner, Harry Tutewiler, began his official inquest on Monday, November 2. Two weeks later, after interviewing over one hundred witnesses, the coroner reached his verdict. He fixed the blame for the accident on B.C. Byers, who wasn't even in Indiana when the accident happened. His office was in Kankakee, Illinois, where he was the chief train dispatcher for the Chicago Division of the CCC and St. L. Railroad. The Indianapolis area was under the jurisdiction of the Chicago Division. The coroner reasoned that Byers had failed to notify J.Q. Hicks, the general yardmaster at Indianapolis, of the two Purdue specials en route to Indianapolis. As a result, without knowing about the approach of the special trains, the yardmaster allowed the coal train to use the main track. No specific rule said the chief dispatcher should notify the local yardmaster of any special trains coming. However, various witnesses testified that the yardmaster was usually informed.

The coroner also found fault with the speed of both trains. He pointed out an Indianapolis city ordinance stating: "No train should run in or through the City of Indianapolis at speeds greater than 4 MPH." Testimony determined that the coal train was backing up at nine miles per hour, while the Purdue special was running at least thirty miles per hour or more.

Another point brought out by the coroner was that there was a specific rule of the railroad that said "trains running between North Indianapolis and the shops (which covered the area where the wreck occurred) must be kept under control and expect to find the track occupied by yard engines." Due to its speed, the Purdue train was not "under control." However, the coroner said that because of orders that the train arrive at Union Station at a specific time, it had to run at a faster than safe speed. He ruled that the train crew wouldn't share the blame for the accident because of this.

Nonetheless, the December 15, 1903 edition of the *Indianapolis News* reported that the railroad company had fired the engineer of the ill-fated train. The same article also revealed that the conductor of the same train was now working for a different railroad. He'd allegedly quit before the company could terminate him.

In December 1903, a Marion County grand jury met to decide whether any criminal charges would come from this case. In its report, on December 24, 1903, no single person was held responsible for the accident. Instead, the report blamed the lack of cooperation between various departments within the railroad company. The report also said, "There is no law in this state by which to charge a man with manslaughter for 'inattention to duty.' Other states have such a law. Whatever unlawful acts were committed in another state are beyond our jurisdiction." That seemed directed at the train dispatcher in Kankakee, Illinois, whom the coroner blamed for the accident.

One result of the crash was that it severely impaired the athletic budgets of both schools. The Indianapolis game was canceled, of course. Purdue had purchased about $800 ($27,092) worth of tickets, and IU had bought about $600 ($20,319) worth of tickets. Fans in the Indianapolis area had bought about $800 ($27,092) worth of tickets. These were advance-sale tickets. Ticket sales at the gate would have added considerably to these figures.

Total expenses for the teams to play in Indianapolis were estimated at $1,000 ($33,865). That amount covered the rental of Washington Park, advertising, ticket printing and other costs.

Most students and alumni didn't seek a refund. However, about half of the Indianapolis fans who'd bought tickets asked for their money back. The amount of money left after refunds wasn't reported. Indiana University agreed that any funds left after expenses should go to Purdue University.

In light of the tragedy, some businesses offered to waive any fees owed them. Washington Park, where the game was to be played, was one such business. Unfortunately, others weren't as generous. For example, a local company had been given a $5 ($169) down payment to rent transportation to convey the Purdue team to the ballpark. The company insisted that Purdue pay the other $7 ($237) still owed, even though the transportation went unused.

Having expenses with no income to offset them greatly affected IU's athletic budget. James Horne, the Indiana University athletic director, said, "We are in desperate straits at Indiana as a result of the loss of receipts on Saturday. The track team cannot be put out this winter, and I do not believe we will have basketball either. So critical is the situation that the baseball and football teams next year will be seriously handicapped. We do feel that Purdue should first be helped. Our first thought, even in our predicament, is for Purdue."

Purdue's football season ended due to the wreck. The team immediately canceled the rest of its games scheduled for 1903. It was believed Purdue would have no football team for at least two or three years because so many members of their current team had been killed or badly injured. That was not the case, however.

One year later, the two schools met again on the football field. In November 1904, they played one game in Indianapolis, which Purdue won. After this game, they decided that playing in neutral territory wasn't worth the trouble it took to arrange. Since then, the schools have met on the football field each year, with games alternating between the two campuses. Since 1925, the winning school has been awarded a trophy called "The Old Oaken Bucket."

There are two memorials on the Purdue campus for victims of the crash. The Memorial Gymnasium, now known as Felix Haas Hall, was dedicated in 1909. The seventeen steps leading up to the entrance commemorate the seventeen lives lost in the 1903 accident.

In 2003, on the one hundredth anniversary of the tragic loss, the school dedicated a tunnel in the football stadium to the people lost in 1903, especially members of the school's football team. Today, the current football team uses this tunnel to enter and leave the stadium.

In Indianapolis, the area where the wreck occurred has undergone major changes. As a result, it looks significantly different than it did in 1903. The railroad tracks and most streets and houses once located near the accident scene are long gone. The construction of Interstate 65 caused the removal of most of them.

Today, the accident's initial point of impact would be located just east of the right-hand, northbound lane of Interstate 65, approximately 150 feet northwest of the intersection of Senate Boulevard and the West Entrance Drive to IU Health Methodist Hospital. The interstate now covers most of the wreck site.

12

PREST-O-LITE AND ITS SERIES
OF CATASTROPHES

The Prest-O-Lite Company was both good and bad for the city of Indianapolis. It was good, because without Prest-O-Lite, there would probably not be an Indianapolis Motor Speedway. And without the speedway, there would be no Indianapolis 500 Mile Race; no one-hundred-plus years of exciting racing; no hosting of the world's largest single-day sporting event; no traditions of generations of families spending days at the track, watching the cars, picnicking and having a good time; no hundreds of thousands of people traveling from all over the world each year to attend the race; no 500 Festival Parade and other related activities. None of this would have happened without Prest-O-Lite.

In addition, the speedway has generated a lot of tax revenue for Indianapolis and Marion County. Just think of all the money spent on food, beverages and overnight accommodations since the track opened in 1909.

But the Prest-O-Lite Company was also bad for the city. In just a few years, the company suffered explosions, fires and a building collapse in three different Indianapolis locations. These incidents caused the deaths of eleven men, injuries to dozens of people and property damage to literally hundreds of buildings.

So, was Prest-O-Lite good or bad? It depends on who you ask. To a fan of the 500? It was good. But ask the families of those killed or injured due to incidents caused by Prest-O-Lite. They'd probably have a different answer.

The Concentrated Acetylene Company was founded in 1904 by Percy Avery, Carl Fisher and James Allison. Mr. Avery invented a process that used compressed acetylene gas to illuminate automobile headlights. However, he needed money to start a company and put his invention to practical use. Fisher and Allison were well-known Indianapolis businessmen who supplied the capital to fund this new venture. Some sources say they invested only $5,000 ($167,421) each.

Then in 1906, Allison and Fisher bought out Mr. Avery's share of the business and became the sole company owners. They changed its name to the Prest-O-Lite Company. Both men became very wealthy from this business venture. And with part of this wealth, Carl Fisher, James Allison and two other partners, Arthur Newby and Frank Wheeler, founded the Indianapolis Motor Speedway Company in the spring of 1909. The first auto races took place in August that same year. The first Indianapolis 500 occurred on May 30, 1911, and it has been held annually since then—except during World War I and World War II.

During the early years of automotive history, automobile headlights were little more than lanterns illuminated by burning kerosene or oil. They helped others see vehicles approaching but didn't provide much illumination for drivers to see ahead.

A set of Prest-O-Lite headlights was much brighter, allowing drivers to see farther down the road. That was obviously a significant factor in safe driving. Prest-O-Lite headlights burned acetylene, producing a flame much brighter than kerosene-fueled headlights.

The acetylene gas was stored in a pressurized brass cylinder, usually mounted on the car's running board. The gas was delivered to the headlights via metal tubing. One cylinder stored enough gas to illuminate a pair of headlights for twenty to forty hours.

To turn these headlights on, drivers had to first start the gas flow to the lights by opening a valve. Then, when they pushed a button mounted on the car's dashboard, a spark lit the gas in the headlights. Presto! As if by magic, there were lights, hence the name Prest-O-Lite.

The brass cylinders of acetylene were easily exchanged when they ran low. Drivers merely sent their empty cylinders back to Prest-O-Lite with a small payment, and the company would send back a freshly refilled cylinder. With the numerous railroad routes and regularly scheduled trains, a Prest-O-Lite customer almost anywhere in the country could send their empty cylinder to the company and get another full one by the next day. That quick turnaround was aided by Prest-O-Lite owning about fifteen refilling facilities nationwide. Many of these out-of-state facilities also experienced explosions, but this chapter only concerns the Prest-O-Lite operations in Indianapolis.

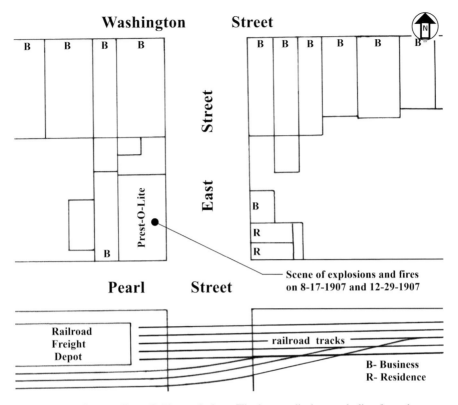

A map of the first two Prest-O-Lite explosions. The brass cylinders exploding from the factory threatened several businesses and two residences. *Map by author.*

Prest-O-Lite's first brush with disaster came on Saturday, August 17, 1907. Just before noon, a loud explosion rattled the neighborhood around East Street, half a block south of Washington Street. The Prest-O-Lite Company's three-story, 40-by-120-foot brick building, located at 20–24 South East Street, was the site of the explosion. There were about twenty-seven employees inside the building at the time of the blast. They all escaped, although a few suffered minor injuries. Three women who were working on the third floor had to flee using a metal ladder mounted on the side of the building. Mayme Clemens escaped uninjured, while Katie Metz suffered bruising and minor lacerations.

Emma Brown, the third woman, was climbing down the ladder when she was startled by another explosion and let go before reaching the bottom rung. A bystander tried unsuccessfully to catch her. However, he at least managed to break her fall, receiving slight injuries as he did so. Miss

Brown sprained her ankle in the incident. As she struggled to limp away from the burning building, a policeman came to her rescue and carried her to safety. There were also five men on the third floor at the time of the explosion. Four of them used the same fire escape the women did after ensuring that all the women were out of the building. The fifth man, Oramel Skinner, braved the flames and ran down the interior stairway and out the front door.

The other injury was to William Luckey, a foreman whose last name proved prophetic. He was working near the location of the initial explosion and had the presence of mind to crawl through flaming debris to turn off the electrical power to the compressor. He knew that without electricity, the gas would stop flowing from the compressor and wouldn't feed the flames. Despite his quick action, the fire rapidly spread out of control. Luckey suffered only minor burns to his face, cuts on his hands and a sprained knee.

The initial explosion was followed by several more. There were so many that one newspaper reported that it sounded like the area was under a "naval bombardment." The flames spread quickly to the second and third floors, helped by the large quantities of highly flammable acetylene gas stored in the building. Numerous gas-filled brass cylinders exploded in the heat, spraying deadly shrapnel in all directions. One cylinder rocketed out of the building and flew 150 feet before making a large hole in the side of a wooden boxcar parked on a railroad siding.

The fire was under control in about an hour. Prest-O-Lite's loss was estimated at $40,000 ($1,268,128), while damage to the building was about $8,000 ($253,626).

Just four months later, on Friday, December 20, 1907, another explosion occurred at the same facility. Shortly after 2:00 p.m., Elmer Jessup was polishing one of the brass cylinders. It had been filled with acetylene and was getting a final burnish before being sent to a customer. There was speculation that friction from the polishing wheel caused the gas cylinder, which possibly had a small, undetected leak, to explode. Mr. Jessup was immediately engulfed in flames and, in a panic, ran in the direction of the front door. In the meantime, the fire quickly spread inside the building.

Mr. Jessup made it out the front door and ran north on the sidewalk; by now, he was a veritable "human torch." Daniel Feaster was driving his buggy on East Street when he saw this horrifying spectacle. He acted quickly, grabbing a blanket he had and knocking Jessup to the ground while smothering the flames. John Vangarder, a Prest-O-Lite employee who was running after Jessup to help him, assisted Feaster. Mr. Vangarder suffered

Top: The first Prest-O-Lite explosion on South Street in August 1907. This photograph was taken from the railyard looking northwest and shows Prest-O-Lite wreathed in smoke, three hoses in operation and a large crowd of spectators. *Author's photograph.*

Bottom: Firefighting efforts in front (the east side) of Prest-O-Lite on South East Street in August 1907. Two hose wagons using Glazier nozzles are shown in the center and right side of the photograph. *The Indianapolis Firefighters Museum.*

burns to his face and hands. Two other employees, Oramel Skinner and Charles Hall, were also injured.

Dr. Edward Katterhenry, whose office was nearby, treated Mr. Jessup after the flames on his body were extinguished. Dr. Katterhenry, in the December 21, 1907 edition of the *Indianapolis Star*, said that Mr. Jessup had "serious burns over most of his body. The only place not burned are the soles of his feet." He also reported that Jessup had no chance of surviving his burns. Elmer Jessup was taken to City Hospital by ambulance. He suffered for about twelve hours before he died on Saturday morning.

Upon seeing Mr. Jessup engulfed in flames and running down the street, someone pulled alarm box no. 83 on the corner of Washington and East Streets. The alarm office sent the first alarm at 2:14 p.m. Once again, fire companies found heavy fire in the Prest-O-Lite building when they arrived. At 2:20 p.m., a second alarm was dispatched.

As firefighters worked to contain the flames, secondary explosions were occurring. One explosion hurled debris across East Street, where it broke a window on the second floor of a residence. After an hour and a half of fighting, the blaze was finally controlled, with damage estimated at $30,000 ($951,096).

Less than a week after this second incident, an Indianapolis city councilman announced he would introduce an ordinance to ban the manufacturing of explosives (including flammable gas) within the city limits. He hoped to force Prest-O-Lite, which had a new facility under construction on South Street, to move its dangerous gas-filling operation beyond the city limits.

The ordinance passed, but Prest-O-Lite and the city reached a compromise. Prest-O-Lite could still use its new facility for refilling cylinders. However, the acetylene gas had to be manufactured outside the city limits and transported in tanks to South Street. It was this manufacturing process that the city considered so dangerous. It felt it would be less hazardous if Prest-O-Lite stored the acetylene in tanks. Unfortunately, this theory was proved to be wrong—in a big way.

Prest-O-Lite moved into its new building a few weeks after that second explosion. This new building, constructed especially for Prest-O-Lite, was located at 229 East South Street. It was 50 by 190 feet, three stories tall and built of reinforced concrete and brick. Each department was separated from the others with brick walls and steel doors. Theoretically, an incident could be confined to one department if something went wrong. The new building was located between Delaware and Alabama Streets on the south side of East South Street.

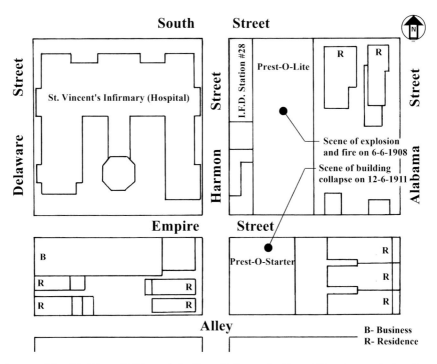

A map of the third Prest-O-Lite and the Prest-O-Starter incidents. Note the proximity of the firehouse and hospital to the Prest-O-Lite factory and the many residences nearby. *Map by author.*

Unfortunately, the company used poor judgment in planning its new site. On the east side of the Prest-O-Lite building were two large private residences. The Indianapolis Fire Department's Station no. 28 adjoined Prest-O-Lite on its west side. Harmon Street (an alley) was on the west side of the fire station, with St. Vincent Hospital immediately west of Harmon Street. The hospital building covered the entire northwest quarter-block from South Street to Empire Street (another alley) and Harmon Street to Delaware Street. The eastern wall of the hospital was just fifty feet from the Prest-O-Lite plant and its dangerous stock of acetylene gas. And Fire Station no. 28 was right between both structures.

The city of Indianapolis had plenty of warnings that this new building was in a bad location. Most apparent were the company's previous explosions in Indianapolis and other cities. In addition, the June 9, 1908 issue of the *Indianapolis Sun* contained an article concerning a letter written by Thomas Markey, a former city councilman. He'd written the letter in February 1908, four months before this third incident occurred. Whether he sent the letter to the city or the newspaper is unclear. In the letter, Markey warned about Prest-O-Lite's proximity to the hospital. He said he'd measured the distance, and according to him, "The wall of the Prest-O-Lite factory is exactly twenty steps from St. Vincent Hospital." He recommended that "the plant should be moved to some less frequented place in the city." He also urged that "it should be placed at least 500 feet from any public building such as a church, school or hospital, and a like distance from any private residences." Sadly, city officials ignored these warnings.

On Saturday, June 6, 1908, it happened again. Prest-O-Lite suffered its third major explosion in Indianapolis in less than one year. However, this time, it damaged more than just Prest-O-Lite property. St. Vincent Hospital and IFD's Station no. 28 were also badly damaged, while hundreds of windows in the area were broken. More importantly, eighteen people were hurt, including a fire department lieutenant who was seriously injured.

The explosion occurred a few minutes after 9:00 a.m. The cause of this explosion was the same as the previous explosion in December 1907. An employee was polishing a gas cylinder when it burst into flames. The fire quickly spread, luckily without causing any injury to the employee this time. But the spreading fire soon involved several storage tanks containing large amounts of acetylene gas. At least two of these tanks exploded. The explosions were so loud that a farmer seven miles east of Indianapolis heard them.

The force of these explosions badly cracked the east and west walls of the fire station and knocked them out of alignment in several places. The front wall of the station was in danger of collapsing, and most of its windows were shattered. In addition, the roof suffered damage when the concussion lifted it into the air and settled it back down out of its original position.

Lieutenant Edward Foullois of Truck no. 2 was standing outside in front of the station at the time of the blast. He was hit and knocked down by parts of the cornice as they fell from the station. He suffered serious head and internal injuries. He was hospitalized and later had to retire due to his injuries. Lieutenant Foullois sued Prest-O-Lite, and in 1909, a jury awarded him $10,000 ($327,484) for his pain and suffering. Several other firefighters were also injured but to lesser degrees.

When the explosion occurred, the concussion forced the doors of the horse stalls inside the fire station to open. The horses were trained to run to the front of the fire apparatus and stand, waiting to be hitched up, when their stall doors opened. This time though, frightened by the explosion, they ran out the open door at the front of the station and continued down the street.

Station no. 28, 125 East South Street. St. Vincent Hospital can be seen on the right. Prest-O-Lite would later be constructed on the left, but this photograph was taken before its construction. A city service ladder truck can be seen in front of station. *The Indianapolis Firefighters Museum.*

To avoid being trampled, firefighters who were attempting to stop them had to step aside. The horses finally stopped a block away and were led back to the station. They were hitched to the fire apparatus, which was then taken outside in case the damaged station collapsed. According to some reports, the noise and concussion from the explosion temporarily deafened the horses.

Flames from the burning gas were showing from several windows after the acetylene tanks inside the Prest-O-Lite building ruptured. As a result, Fire Chief Charles Coots immediately called for a second alarm upon his arrival. However, the building's compartmentalized design and the fire-resistant materials used in its construction limited the spread of the flames within Prest-O-Lite. Once the gas burned away, there was very little fire inside the building. Consequently, not much damage was done to either Prest-O-Lite or its contents. That was certainly not the case with the fire station, the hospital and hundreds of other structures in the area.

All the Prest-O-Lite workers escaped, though there were minor injuries. Otto Hoffmeister, William Hutchinson and John Vangarder suffered burns as they fled the flames by running down a stairway. Another employee, Albert Lemrod, couldn't reach the stairs because of the fire. He had to jump out of a second-story window to escape and suffered a broken leg.

Several people in the area were injured while simply going about their daily business. Mary Quinlan, who lived next door to the Prest-O-Lite building, was working in her backyard when the explosion occurred. She was hit in the head by falling debris and was dazed but otherwise uninjured. Another neighbor, Louis Riehl, suffered cuts when all of his home's windows blew in. He wasn't seriously injured. Charles Hartman was driving by on South Street when the explosion occurred. The force of the blast knocked him from his wagon, slightly injuring him. His horse was startled and ran for several blocks, still pulling the wagon.

At the time of the explosion, Bernard Lada was pasting posters on a fence in the area. He was struck in the head by a brick and knocked down. Somewhat dazed, he didn't realize that he'd been injured. He finished what he was doing and started walking to another area of town to put up more posters. He became dizzy and fainted while waiting to cross a nearby intersection. After seeing him fall, a policeman went to his assistance and saw that he was injured. An ambulance took Lada to his home. A doctor found heavy bruising on Lada's head and speculated that he may have suffered a skull fracture. Another victim was Floy Miles, a young woman who was walking nearby on a sidewalk when the explosion occurred. She was thrown against a lamppost by the force of the blast and suffered slight injuries.

St. Vincent Hospital suffered damage estimated at $3,000 ($97,177). A roof gable on the east side of the building collapsed into the fourth floor, but the rest of the roof was mostly undamaged. Almost all of the building's windows were shattered, including some stained-glass windows in the chapel. The explosion was so violent that shards of broken window glass were embedded in the walls of some rooms. Fortunately, there were no injuries from this flying glass. Many of the rooms had plaster dislodged from their walls and ceilings.

There were several injuries in the hospital. Luckily, none were severe. Albert Brinkhouse was the only patient injured. He suffered bruising and some shock. The hospital employees who sustained injuries were Sister Cephas, who had cuts on her hands; Lela Dowler, who had a sprained shoulder; and Jacob Demmerly, Lizzie Ryan and Nellie Conner, all of whom suffered scrapes and bruises.

The damage caused by the explosion was not confined to the buildings in the immediate area. Hundreds of homes and businesses for several blocks around Prest-O-Lite had their windows shattered. There were claims of cracked and broken windows from as far as half a mile away. Many were large display windows in downtown stores.

Later that day, Thomas Winterrowd, the city's building inspector, checked the damage at Station no. 28. He announced that the building, although badly damaged, was safe and still able to function as a fire station. However, heavy timbers had to be brought in to shore up and brace parts of the building. A "temporary roof" was also installed over the station's damaged roof.

Incredibly, the station continued in service, held together by various braces and shoring, for another two years. Then in June 1910, someone reported that the station's walls were at risk of collapsing, so Mr. Winterrowd inspected the station again. This time, he agreed that the station was in dangerous condition. As a result, the structure was condemned and finally closed on June 27, 1910.

This latest explosion was Prest-O-Lite's proverbial "third strike, and you're out"—out of Indianapolis, that is. City officials finally forced the company to move its gas refilling operations outside the city limits. So, it relocated that part of its operations to what later became the town of Speedway while still retaining ownership of its downtown building.

Unfortunately, that third explosion in June 1908 wasn't the end of Prest-O-Lite's string of catastrophes in downtown Indianapolis. In fact, the worst was yet to come.

In late 1911, a new building was under construction immediately south of the Prest-O-Lite building (the one involved in the third blast) located at 229 East South Street.

The reinforced concrete structure was being built for the Prest-O-Starter Company, a division of the Prest-O-Lite Company. A Prest-O-Starter was a starting system drivers could buy for their automobiles. In those days, vehicles were started by turning a crank at the front of the engine by hand. Unfortunately, that could sometimes be dangerous. Many people suffered broken arms or wrists when the motor unexpectedly fired and violently spun the crank around. Hand cranking was also inconvenient. It meant the driver had to be outside of their vehicles to start them, no matter the weather conditions—rain, snow, heat, cold, et cetera.

The Prest-O-Starter eliminated the danger and inconvenience of starting vehicles from the outside. It did this by allowing drivers to start their cars while they remained inside—something we take for granted now. Unlike today's starters, which use an electric motor to crank the engine, the Prest-O-Starter used acetylene gas. According to the company's advertisements: "A measure of acetylene gas is pumped from the Prest-O-Lite Tank into the cylinders [of your engine]. Touch your spark, and the engine starts." The cost was $20 ($648) for a four-cylinder engine and $25 ($810) for a six-cylinder.

The Prest-O-Starter didn't remain in business very long. Electric starters—the same basic system used today—quickly became the norm and made the company obsolete.

A new concept called a "flat slab, mushroom system" was used to construct Prest-O-Starter's new building. An article in the *Indianapolis Star* on December 3, 1911, described the construction process: "This feature is new in Indianapolis and applies principally to the construction of the floors. Through a process of laying the concrete and by means of an enlarged cap at the top of columns supporting the floors, less material is used, and the efficiency is greater."

The new building cost $30,000 ($941,084) and was seventy by eighty-eight feet in size. The original plans called for it to be a two-story structure, with plans to add a third floor sometime in the future. However, after construction began, the owners decided to add the third story while the building was still under construction instead of waiting until later. The building's architect gave the contractors revised plans, and construction proceeded.

On Wednesday, December 6, 1911, shortly after 1:00 p.m., the workers were just returning from their lunch hour. The general contractor had seventy-five men on the job site. Some subcontractors were also working, but the exact number of these men was undetermined.

The men were beginning to resume work when suddenly, there was a loud crash as the center portion of the roof and much of the third story collapsed into the bottom floors. Some reports estimated that about forty to fifty men were inside the structure at the time of the collapse.

Unable to escape, over a dozen men were buried under tons of concrete, rebar and other debris. Not caught in the initial collapse, more victims were injured when they were forced to jump from windows to escape.

The fire department was dispatched but found only a minor blaze caused by an overturned stove that set fire to wood debris. As some firefighters quickly dealt with that, others began search, rescue and body recovery operations.

Indianapolis newspapers were filled with stories of close calls and tragedies. For example, a man later identified as Angus Dixon was heard faintly calling for help from under an enormous pile of debris. A large slab of concrete and other debris had trapped him. Luckily, the slab wasn't crushing him, but it needed to be moved before firefighters could free him.

He actively participated in his own rescue by telling firefighters and other rescuers where to place various jacks and hoists to their best advantage. They made an opening large enough to free him, but Mr. Dixon still couldn't escape because other debris was trapping his feet and legs. A doctor reached through the opening and gave him an injection for his pain. Finally, firefighters freed Dixon after he'd been trapped for over three hours. They took him next door to St. Vincent Hospital, where he was treated for leg and foot injuries. Unfortunately, after undergoing the amputations of both legs, Mr. Dixon died four days later.

Elmer Simmons, a hod carrier, was working on the second floor. Quoted in the *Indianapolis Star* on December 7, 1911, he reported that initially, he heard loud creaks from above and below him. Continuing the account, he said: "And the next thing I knew, the whole building began to shake. A big hole opened in the center. I attempted to reach a window and escape to the ground by jumping, but the floor sank too quickly. I jumped into the huge opening which spread before me in the central part of the building. Down I went with the wreckage!" Mr. Simmons survived with only a scalp laceration and injuries to one hand, both caused by debris falling on him.

R.F. Jones was a carpenter at the site. He said in the same article that "suddenly, there was a crash and a boom, like a cannon. I was working alongside Millard Headley and Oscar Bailey. We all three went down together. I saw them on each side of me as I fell!" Jones survived with just a cut on his leg. Bailey was seriously injured, while Headley did not survive.

A large crowd of spectators quickly gathered, and many men came out of this crowd to assist in the rescues. There were so many good Samaritans that the police finally had to clear the site of everyone except police and fire personnel. They then allowed men with specialized construction skills to assist as needed. Meanwhile, many of the wives and children of the men who were working at the site crowded the scene, attempting to learn the fate of their loved ones.

As night fell, some men who were known to have been working at the site were still unaccounted for. Officials ordered electric lights to illuminate the scene as the recovery of bodies continued.

The December 7, 1911 edition of the *Indianapolis Star* reported conflicting theories concerning a possible cause for the collapse. First, Harry Wilson, an engineer at St. Vincent Hospital, told the paper that he'd noticed that the west wall of the new building had developed a prominent "bulge" over the last few days. He said that he had pointed this out to several workers. The workers told him that they would inform their supervisor of the bulge.

On the other hand, Edward R. Wolf of Wolf and Ewing, the general contractor, said this in the same article: "As to the bulging of the wall, there is nothing to that statement. If the wall bulged, I was not aware of it. But I believe there was no bulge there, or it would have been noticed." Later, in testimony before the coroner, Wolf blamed the collapse on an excavation done for sewer work.

The concrete pillars on the third floor, which were designed to hold the roof structure, had been poured on Saturday, four days before the collapse. There was speculation that the concrete used in these pillars had not been allowed to cure properly. The weather had been cold—temperatures had been below freezing—and this could have affected the curing process of the concrete. In addition, contractors had brought large beams and other roofing materials to the third floor in preparation for building the roof. The weight of these materials added to the stress of the recently poured concrete.

There were immediate calls to ban this type of construction. Officials made various investigations, but ultimately, it wasn't outlawed. Instead, builders who were utilizing the "flat slab, mushroom system" learned to plan their schedules so that construction could occur when the temperatures would not hamper the curing of the concrete.

Sadly, the collapse took the lives of ten men. In addition, more than twenty-five men were injured, some seriously. On December 31, 1911, a

Marion County grand jury gave their report. They found no violation of any law and placed no blame on anyone. Instead, they recommended that the city update its ordinances regarding reinforced concrete construction.

Ironically, another worker was killed in a similar incident just four months later on April 15, 1912. A building that was under construction at Market and Davidson Streets had part of its roof and fourth floor collapse after wooden forms were removed from the recently poured concrete roof. It was speculated that freezing weather had also affected the curing time for that concrete. This construction had no connection with the Prest-O-Starter project.

Carl Fisher and James Allison sold Prest-O-Lite to the Union Carbide Corporation for $9,000,000 ($209,538,281) in 1917. It was certainly a good return on an initial investment of only $5,000 each ($167,421).

Today, a parking lot occupies the site of the Prest-O-Lite Company's South East Street location, the scene of the first two explosions. On East South Street, the sites of the Prest-O-Lite and Prest-O-Starter buildings, IFD's Station no. 28 and St. Vincent Hospital are now covered by buildings that house the Irsay Family YMCA and the CityWay/Franciscan Health facility, along with their parking lot.

In the town of Speedway, there are still reminders of the Prest-O-Lite Company. Presto Avenue was named in its honor. Appropriately enough, Fisher Avenue and Allison Avenue are nearby. The town also has schools named for Carl Fisher and James Allison. In addition, there is a thoroughfare in Speedway named Polco Street. Polco stands for <u>P</u>rest-<u>O</u>-Lite <u>Co</u>mpany.

13

THE IRVINGTON RAILROAD ACCIDENT

A passenger train was traveling from Cincinnati to Indianapolis early on November 13, 1912. Tragically, it collided head on with a freight train before reaching its destination. The freight train had been parked on a siding on the east side of Indianapolis to allow the passenger train to hurry by as it journeyed toward Union Station in downtown Indianapolis. One of the freight train's crew members opened the switch, allowing the train to go back on the sidetrack. After that, however, they failed to close the switch to reopen the main track. In the early morning darkness, no one noticed the error.

The collision that followed resulted in the deaths of fifteen persons and injuries to dozens of others. All of these deaths occurred on the passenger train. There was an immediate outcry to learn how this accident happened.

The passenger train left Cincinnati at 11:25 p.m. on Tuesday, November 12, and was due in Indianapolis at 2:38 a.m. on November 13. The train was running about forty miles per hour but was an hour late at the time of the accident. Following its stop in Indianapolis, the train was scheduled to travel to Chicago, arriving at 7:40 a.m. But it would never make that trip to Chicago.

At 1:15 a.m., on Wednesday, November 13, the freight train, with twenty-six heavily loaded cars and four empty ones, left Indianapolis, bound for Hamilton, Ohio, north of Cincinnati. That train's crew had instructions to proceed to Julietta, Indiana, a small community on the Marion-Hancock County line. There, they were to pull onto a sidetrack and wait for the passenger train to pass. However, as the train approached the Arlington Avenue siding, the conductor calculated that they wouldn't have time to reach Julietta before the passenger train. So, he ordered the train to stop. It then backed onto the Arlington Avenue siding to await the passenger train. That siding was on the south side of Irvington, Indiana, a small east side suburban community that was annexed into Indianapolis in 1902. Both trains were operated by the Cincinnati, Hamilton and Dayton Railroad Company.

In later testimony, the freight train's crew estimated they had been waiting for twenty-five to thirty-five minutes when they saw the headlight of the passenger train approaching. The freight train had backed into the siding, which meant that its locomotive was facing southeast, the same direction from which the other train was coming. The train's conductor and another crewman were in the caboose, while the engineer, fireman and head brakeman were all in the locomotive. While waiting for the passenger train, the crew members in the locomotive were killing time, smoking and making small talk.

It all happened in an instant. Instead of speeding by the freight train on the main track, the passenger train's locomotive suddenly veered onto the siding, hitting the freight train's locomotive head on. There was a tremendous crash as the two locomotives slammed together. They both reared up as the momentum of the lighter passenger train hit the heavily loaded, parked freight train. The steam boilers of both locomotives exploded, spraying scalding water over a wide area. A tank of natural gas that was used to provide lighting in the passenger cars also exploded, adding to the tremendous noise of the crash. The escaping gas quickly caught fire, and flames soon spread among the wreckage.

The great locomotives settled back to the earth as the forward velocity of the passenger train caused massive carnage behind it. The freight train, other than its destroyed locomotive, was relatively undamaged.

But that was not the case with the passenger train. Its locomotive was also terribly damaged. In addition, the locomotive's tender, immediately behind, smashed into its rear, instantly killing the engineer and fireman inside the cab. That also caused the tender's load of coal to fly into the air. It all came raining down on the wrecks of both locomotives. Next in line behind the tender was the U.S. Mail car. It had a modern design and was made of metal rather than wood. That helped protect the men who were working inside. Of the four mail clerks in the car, only one required hospitalization. The other clerks, although injured, were able to remain on duty, sorting mail in the damaged car for several hours after the accident.

The cars behind the mail car were mostly of wooden construction and did not fare as well. The forward momentum caused these cars to crash against each other. The worst incident happened when the first Pullman car "telescoped" into the combination baggage and smoking car. Telescoping occurs when the frame of one railroad car overrides the other, and the two vehicles slide together, one inside the other, like the tubes of a telescope as it collapses. In this case, the two fit together so perfectly that only about fifteen or twenty feet of the Pullman car was visible, sticking out the rear of the baggage and smoking car. Almost all of the deaths—besides those of the crew in the cab—occurred in these two cars.

The engineer of the passenger train, William Sharkey, thirty-six, died in the wreck, along with Carl Berg, twenty-two, the fireman on the train. Their bodies were trapped in the tangled rubble for several hours before they were recovered. Sharkey had just returned to work a few days before the wreck. He had been off duty since he was badly scalded in May 1912 when a steam line burst inside the cab of a locomotive he was driving. Carl Berg, the passenger train fireman, had recently promised his family that this would be his final trip. After that, he planned to leave the railroad and start a new career. But sadly, fate had different plans, and this became the last trip he would ever

This photograph from the *Hammond* (IN) *Lake County Times* shows the Pullman car telescoped almost entirely inside the combination baggage/smoking car. *Courtesy of the* Lake County Times.

make. Irvie Wiggins, forty-five, the passenger train conductor, also died in the wreck. He'd been a railroad employee for almost thirty years. His elderly mother lived with Wiggins, his wife and their two daughters. Upon learning of Wiggins's death, his mother and wife were so overcome with grief that a doctor was called to treat them. Finally, Horace White, thirty-five, a brakeman on the passenger train, also died in the crash. He'd been employed by the railroad for forty years and, although he'd been involved in several previous wrecks, had never before been injured. These four men were the only crew members who lost their lives. The other eleven victims were passengers.

Christian Imholte, forty, was a cabinetmaker from Cincinnati. He'd been in ill health for a while, and some relatives—Albert Allen, thirty, and his wife, Clara, twenty-seven—had traveled from Los Angeles to bring him back to California with them. They felt the warmer climate would help him regain his strength. But sadly, all three of them perished in the wreck.

Benjamin Boyle, nineteen, of Cincinnati was a proofreader. He was traveling to Chicago to begin a new job when he died in the accident. Unfortunately, Boyle provided the primary source of income for his aged mother.

Another victim, Charles Grundhoefer, forty-five, lived with his wife and four sons in Cincinnati, where he was a carpenter. According to the November 14, 1912 *Indianapolis Star*, Mr. Grundhoefer left his house on the evening of November 12 without telling anyone where he was going. He'd left home this way a few times in the past. However, this time, he would never return.

Joseph Palmer, thirty, worked for the Louisville and Nashville Railroad. He was from Etowah, Tennessee, and was traveling on the CH&DRR on a pass issued by the L&NRR.

The remaining victims were all from one family. Although this wreck had many tragic stories, this was the most heartbreaking. Clifton Chaney and his family were from Jackson, Kentucky. Chaney was twenty-five years old and was hoping to make a new life for his family. They were traveling to Wisconsin, where he was to begin a new job.

Tragically, his entire family died in the crash: Mr. Chaney's twenty-four-year-old wife, Julia; their two-year-old daughter, Lydia; their five-year-old son, Chester; his thirteen-year-old brother, Charles; and his sixty-one-year-old father, John. Clifton Chaney was the only survivor of all those traveling with him to Wisconsin. He was severely injured and, because of that, wasn't informed of his family's deaths for several days. He was finally released from the hospital three weeks later. An article in the November 15, 1912 edition of the *Indianapolis Star* noted, "The Chaneys were poor but were hard workers." It also said they had saved some money and purchased an interest in a lumber company in Wisconsin.

In a further twist of fate, the paper reported that Clifton Chaney had attempted to purchase accident insurance when he bought his family's train tickets. However, the agent was busy at the time, so they boarded the train without buying the insurance. The policy would have paid $30,000 ($921,680) if he'd obtained it.

Several other people on the passenger train were injured—some quite seriously. For example, Hugh Kemp, thirty-six, received head, shoulder and leg injuries. Although newspaper reports listed his injuries as "probably fatal," he survived. W.J. Filer, twenty-four, received head and internal injuries and was in serious condition. Clifton Chaney's severe injuries were previously mentioned. Harry Sell, twenty-seven, and Fred Emberton, twenty-six, had less severe injuries. These five men were all passengers.

Besides the injured crew members already mentioned, Burton Jones, thirty-seven, a mail sorter; J.C. Skillman, sixty-four, a baggage handler; and J.W. Jefferson, a porter, were also injured passenger train crewmen. Mr. Jefferson's condition was listed as "probably fatal," but he did survive.

The three crewmen in the cab of the parked freight train were all injured. Willis York, twenty-six, the engineer, leaped from the cab of his locomotive just as the passenger train hit. He received burns when scalding water from the exploding boilers sprayed him as he jumped. He also had minor cuts from landing on a barbed wire fence. The fireman on the freight train, Fred Hutchenson, twenty-six, was also severely burned by the boiler explosion. He was near death for several days but finally survived. Carl Gross, twenty-seven, the head brakeman, suffered a badly broken leg. As the investigation began, he would bear the brunt of the blame for the accident.

The coroner determined that the crash occurred thirty seconds after 3:17 a.m. He was able to do so because a watch belonging to Carl Berg, the fireman of the passenger train, was found in the wreckage. Berg died in the crash, and his broken watch showed the exact time at which the crash occurred. Railroad crewmembers were known for having accurate timepieces because their jobs depended on precise timekeeping.

The Indianapolis Fire Department responded from Station no. 25 at 5430 East Washington Street in Irvington. Two horse-drawn apparatus, a hose wagon and a combination chemical engine/ladder truck, responded. The department also sent a motorized manpower squad and a motorized hose wagon from its headquarters station downtown at 250 Massachusetts Avenue. These vehicles and the combination engine from Irvington carried chemical tanks. These were thirty-five- or forty-five-gallon water containers from which a chemical reaction expelled water through a hose.

In an article in the November 14, 1912 edition of the *Indianapolis Star*, Indianapolis Fire Chief Charles Coots credited the motorized apparatus's fast responses with saving lives. He said that the apparatus from the Irvington station had been struggling to control the fire before the other crews arrived. Once they were on the scene, the fire was extinguished before it could reach the people trapped in the wreckage.

The tremendous noise of the collision woke people up and alerted the entire neighborhood that a bad accident had occurred. As people learned the extent of the injuries, they opened their homes and assisted the injured. However, that also caused some problems. For instance, the fireman on the passenger train, Fred Hutchenson, was scalded by hot water. He was carried to a nearby house and treated there. Unfortunately, the authorities were unaware of this, and for several hours, they thought he was still lying in the wreckage. As a result, they wasted time searching for him.

The accident caused a flurry of excitement in Indianapolis. As people learned of what happened, they rushed to the scene. The *Indianapolis Star*'s November 14 edition estimated that more than fifteen thousand people had viewed the accident scene during daylight hours on November 13. It estimated the crowd was never smaller than five thousand at any one time. Spectators watched as crews cleared wreckage from the tracks and removed the unfortunate victims. The paper described: "Women, many with babies in their arms, stood in the cold and in a drizzling rain, waiting to see the bodies of the unfortunate Engineer and Fireman, which were among the last to be removed." They also described a search for souvenirs as "spectators attempted to obtain twisted pieces of iron, brass, or polished wood on which to cut or file the date as a memoir of the wreck."

All of these spectators caused numerous traffic jams. The paper said, "Every street within a half-mile radius of the wreck was blocked with automobiles." Other persons traveled to the scene by streetcar. There were so many spectators that the streetcar company added extra cars to accommodate them. That was still not enough. Consequently, as the spectators left Irvington in the afternoon, several thousand had to endure long waits to board streetcars to take them back downtown.

About twenty-four hours after this accident, a sixty-year-old man was hit by a different train and killed. That accident occurred on the same tracks, close to the scene of the previous day's collision. The man lived a few blocks away on South Berry Street. The newspaper article about this accident noted that the same household on South Berry Street had experienced two other tragic deaths within the past year. About six months previously, a nine-month-old infant died in the home due to accidental drowning, and a few months before that, a sixteen-year-old male resident of that same address was struck and killed by a train while walking along the same train tracks.

The fatal 1912 collision happened almost exactly ten years after a similar accident killed four men and injured ten. That accident occurred on November 8, 1902, when a CH&D freight train, inbound toward Indianapolis, hit a work train going east on the same track. This happened about one and a half miles west of the scene of the 1912 accident. All of the men who were killed and injured in this incident were railroad employees. The 1902 accident resulted from an error by a railroad dispatcher. He allowed both trains to use the same track while telling each they had a clear track. As a result, the two trains were going at high speeds. They collided head on in foggy conditions while on a curve, further limiting their visibility.

Dr. Charles Durham, the Marion County coroner, began an inquest into the 1912 accident the next day, November 14. Carl Gross, the head brakman of the freight train, was one of the first witnesses called. In the first few hours after the accident, CH&D Railroad officials had blamed him for not closing the switch.

Mr. Gross initially accepted the blame but then recanted his statement. He claimed that when he took responsibility, he'd been under the influence of an anesthetic given to him because of a broken leg suffered in the accident. Due to this medication, he didn't realize what he'd said.

At the inquest, Gross described his actions on the morning of the wreck:

> Our train stopped on the main track, and I got off and opened the switch to the side track. The conductor then told me to go down the track in case the passenger train came along before the freight train was clear. I had a lantern and flag if I needed to flag down the passenger train and was about 400 feet down the tracks. The freight signaled me with their whistle that they were clear, and I returned. When I passed the switch, it appeared alright [closed to allow the other train to pass], but my lantern wasn't very good. I don't see how I could possibly close the switch and be flagging the passenger train at the same time when I was 400 feet from the switch!

Further questioning of Mr. Gross revealed that the switch was locked when he first found it, but it had no signal light to indicate its locked/unlocked status. He said that when he returned to the train, he was in the cab of the freight train along with other crew members. One of them asked him if the switch looked alright, and he said it looked OK to him. Unfortunately, no other crewman got off the train to make sure it was closed. Shortly after this, the collision occurred.

The conductor of the train, Patrick Hines, was interviewed next. He corroborated Gross's story that he'd sent him down the track in case the passenger train needed to be flagged down. Hines testified that, immediately after the accident, he realized the switch hadn't been closed. He then exclaimed to crewman Everett Cox, "My God, Ed, what have you done?" Cox replied, "Paddy, I met Carl Gross and Will York [the train's brakeman and engineer] coming from the switch. They both told me the switch was thrown [closed], and I took their word for it and returned to the caboose."

Patrick Hines was also questioned about the switch's operation. He said the switch functioned properly, except that its indicator light was out. He intended to report this malfunction to the trainmaster at Morristown, Indiana, the train's next scheduled stop.

Dr. Durham, the coroner, asked the freight train's engineer, Willis York, about certain railroad rules, specifically the rule reading, "In case the brakeman is busy elsewhere, it is the duty of the engineer to close a switch or to see that it is closed." The coroner felt that this rule meant that the engineer was responsible for the switch, since the conductor had ordered Brakeman Carl Gross to go further down the track. However, Engineer York declined to answer the question. York testified that he had asked Gross if the switch was closed, and he said Gross answered, "Yes, the switch is closed all right." However, Gross told the coroner that he responded to York's question by saying, "Apparently, the switch was closed."

Engineer Willis York also described what happened just before the accident. He said that as the passenger train approached, its headlight illuminated the area, and he realized the switch was in the wrong position. Knowing a collision was imminent, he jumped just as the trains hit.

In mid-December 1912, Coroner Durham released his verdict, which said that engineer Willis York was mainly responsible for the accident. He made this decision because of the railroad rule saying the engineer was responsible for closing the switch if the brakeman was busy. However, he also noted that the brakeman, Carl Gross, was partly responsible, because he'd been careless.

At about the same time, the Railroad Commission of Indiana released its report on the accident. That report also blamed York and Gross, with York again being held primarily responsible.

On December 31, 1912, partly due to these reports, the Marion County grand jury issued involuntary manslaughter indictments to sixteen persons. Those indicted included not just the Engineer, Willis York, and Head Brakeman, Carl Gross, but they also included fourteen high-ranking railroad executives. The officials ranged from the president and board of directors to the local superintendent.

This shocked the entire railroad industry. No top executives of an American railroad company had ever faced indictment due to an accident. Could railroad officials be held criminally responsible if their railroad hired someone who later did something that caused death or injury?

In 1911, the Indiana legislature passed a law that said by January 1, 1912, any railroad operating within the state needed a block signal system installed on its tracks. An automatic block signal system is used to safely control the movement of trains over a section, or block, of a track using signals alongside the railroad track. This same type of system is still in use.

The section of railroad track between Indianapolis and Glenwood, Indiana, a small town in Rush County, still needed to have the new system installed at the time of the accident. That was initially why criminal indictments were issued for the railroad executives. Later, it was learned that the state had given the railroad additional time to install the signal system. The railroad alleged that even if block signals had been installed, they would not have prevented the accident.

At the end of May 1913, the Marion County prosecutor dismissed the indictments issued to the railroad executives. At the same time, new charges, again for involuntary manslaughter, were issued for Willis York, the engineer, and Carl Gross, the head brakeman.

However, the prosecutor dismissed these charges by the end of 1914. It was determined that there was not enough evidence for a conviction of either man.

The former head brakeman, Carl Gross, filed suit against the railroad on February 27, 1913. He charged that it was negligent because the switch was not closed, it was unlit and the passenger train was speeding. He asked for damages of $25,000 ($752,550).

In October 1913, a jury awarded Carl Gross $3,000 ($90,306). However, two months later, the railroad company appealed this verdict. Subsequently, the Indiana Appellate Court reversed the decision on February 25, 1916. The attorneys for Gross were overruled when they requested a rehearing in June 1916. After that, they petitioned to have the Indiana Supreme Court hear the case. Their petition was granted, and the court heard the case in

January 1917. The supreme court upheld the original ruling. Accordingly, it awarded Carl Gross $3,000, plus the interest accrued since the lower court's initial ruling on October 28, 1913.

Today, the main track of the railroad is still in everyday use. It's located on Irvington's south side, very close to the intersection of Arlington and English Avenues. Many of the homes in nearby neighborhoods were there at the time of the wreck. However, the siding where the accident occurred has since been removed.

14

THE COLFAX HALL APARTMENT FIRE

O n April 19, 1917, an explosion and fire in a downtown apartment building caused the deaths of six people. What was the cause of this tragic incident? Merely some motion picture film that caught fire in the building's basement.

How could something as simple as movie film start a fire? All film begins with a "film base," which is the transparent portion of the film. Then a photosensitive emulsion is placed on top of this base. When a length of film is exposed to light within a movie camera, each frame becomes a slightly different photograph. After the film is developed and shown through a projector, it becomes a motion picture.

Motion picture film and X-ray film were both very flammable. That was due to their film base, which was made from nitrocellulose from the late 1800s until the early 1950s. Unfortunately, nitrocellulose is highly flammable. It can be ignited by almost anything, from an open flame to a spark produced by friction or static electricity. And once ignited, it burns with an explosive force while also giving off toxic fumes. Another danger is the potassium nitrate used in the manufacturing of nitrocellulose. Nitrates contain oxygen. That means nitrocellulose can burn even when completely submerged in water. Because of this, a fire involving a nitrocellulose film base can be challenging to extinguish.

Another danger from a historical standpoint is that nitrocellulose degrades over time. After many years, the film becomes soft, sticky and completely unviewable while remaining highly flammable. As a result, many old and historical motion pictures have been lost forever when their last remaining copy completely degraded. The Film Foundation, a nonprofit organization dedicated to the preservation of films, estimates that half of all films made before 1950 and 90 percent of those made before 1929 are lost forever. And degradation of their nitrocellulose film base was the main reason these films were lost.

A much safer type of film base became available in the early 1900s. This so-called safety film used cellulose acetate instead of nitrocellulose as its film base. However, this film was used primarily for family movies shot at home. Professionally produced Hollywood movies shown in theaters continued to use the dangerously flammable type of film base until the early 1950s.

There have been several fires in which deaths occurred due to the burning of nitrocellulose film. One example was the fire at the Cleveland Clinic, a private hospital founded in 1921 in Cleveland, Ohio. On May 15, 1929, a fire occurred in the hospital's X-ray storage room. An estimated three to four tons of X-rays were held in the room. They caught fire, possibly from the heat of a nearby light bulb, and burned furiously. Unfortunately, the fire also produced large amounts of toxic gas. These poisonous fumes spread quickly throughout the four-story hospital and caused 123 deaths and 92 injuries.

Other tragic incidents involving film included an 1897 fire in Paris, France, that started when the film in a movie projector caught fire. The resulting blaze killed 126 people. Even sadder were the deaths of 71 children in 1929 at a theater in Paisley, Scotland. To be fair, most of the deaths in these incidents were caused by panic as people tried to escape the flames. But in both cases, the initial fire was caused by film burning.

These highly flammable films were also the reason that movie theaters were required to have an enclosed projection room. These rooms were constructed from noncombustible materials to contain any fire within them. Sadly, the projectionist sometimes became trapped in the room by fire or was killed by the deadly fumes produced when the film burned. An article in a 1936 issue of a trade magazine for movie projectionists estimated that an average of one projectionist every eighteen days was killed somewhere in America due to this type of incident.

Unfortunately, Indianapolis also suffered a tragic incident in which people died due to the burning of nitrocellulose film. On April 19, 1917, an explosion quickly followed by a large volume of fire occurred at the Colfax apartment building. It was on the southwest corner of Meridian and Tippecanoe Streets and had an address of 320 North Meridian.

The complex had two buildings, Colfax Hall and the Colfax building. Colfax Hall was a three-story, brick, forty-by-one-hundred-foot building with a basement. There were twelve apartments on each of the first two floors. The entire third floor contained an auditorium that several clubs and organizations used for meetings.

At the front (east side) of the apartment building was the three-story brick Colfax building that measured about thirty-five by fifty-five feet. Originally a private, single-family residence, it was now being used as an office building. Colfax Hall had been constructed at the rear of the former mansion in what was once the home's backyard. The two buildings were connected.

The front part of the basement under the apartment building had storage space for use by tenants. The Oxon Chemical Company rented the rest of the basement. This company, owned by Louis R. Sereinsky, bought old movies and X-ray films and then processed them to reclaim silver from the emulsion. The company first softened the emulsion by soaking the film in a vat of hot water. Next, the softened film would be run through an electrically powered scraper. The scraped emulsion would then be treated with chemicals to isolate its silver content. One report estimated that one thousand feet of movie film would yield about a half-ounce of silver. In that era, most movies shown in theaters were one thousand to four thousand feet long. X-ray film was estimated to produce about twenty-eight to thirty-five ounces of silver per one hundred pounds of film. In 1917, the average price for an ounce of silver was $0.89 ($20.72).

The city inspected the location of the Oxon Chemical Company in 1916. Jacob Hilkene, the Indianapolis City Building Commissioner, warned the apartment building's owners and the chemical company about the dangers of storing film in a residential building. Mr. Hilkene added, "If I had any law to act upon, such a dangerous business would not be operated underneath an apartment building. The only thing I could do is what I did. That was to demand that Sereinsky put in a fireproof vault built of brick and concrete, in which I ordered him to keep the films. He promised me that he would only have films outside the vault while they were being processed." Hilkene said, "There is no satisfactory law or ordinance giving the city the proper control of such a situation. There are a number of places where films are stored, and some of them we know nothing about because we have no way to track them. The use of any building where people live should be prohibited for film storage."

The chemical company did build a brick vault in the basement, as ordered by the building inspector. However, the company wasn't properly

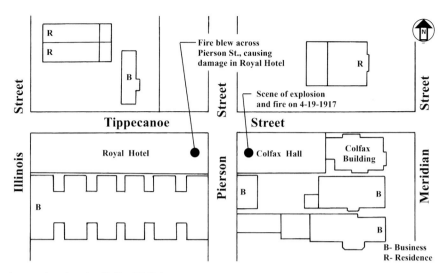

A map showing the Colfax Hall Apartment fire scene. Meridian Street had many large mansions along it. By 1917, several former mansions were being used to house businesses. *Map by author.*

using it at the time of the fire—at least not in the way the inspector had envisioned. Following the fire, authorities found only a few barrels inside the vault. Meanwhile, at least twenty-five barrels, now filled with only ashes and scorched film reels, were found outside the vault. The same vault—had the barrels have been inside when the fire occurred—would have kept the flames contained safely within.

When confronted with this fact, Mr. Sereinsky first claimed that only eight barrels of films were outside the vault. When informed that there were at least twenty-five, Sereinsky changed his story and said, "What I meant was that only eight of the barrels were completely full of film. The other barrels were just partly full." He claimed the barrels were outside the vault because the company was preparing to ship them out. Investigators estimated that the full barrels each contained about two hundred pounds of film.

Fire investigators never learned what caused the films to ignite. There was no question that the fire originated in the rear of the basement, where the film was stored. However, despite several theories, what caused the film to ignite was never determined.

One cause may have been the film-scraping machine. Investigators found its switch in the "on" position, but Mr. Sereinsky claimed that no one had worked in the basement for several hours before the fire. In addition, the scraper had been installed without the knowledge of the building inspector.

This meant the installation had never been inspected to ensure it was installed safely. Sparks from this machine could have started the fire.

Investigators also found some barrels of scrap films close to steam pipes. The heat from these pipes may have hastened the decomposition of the film. The subsequent gas produced as the film degraded could have somehow ignited. Authorities also theorized that spontaneous combustion could have been the culprit.

Whatever the cause, at about 6:45 p.m. on April 19, 1917, a massive explosion occurred, quickly followed by a large volume of flames blowing out of the basement. The weather was warm that April evening. Many of the apartment windows were open to let in cooling breezes. Unfortunately, the concussion broke many windows that weren't already open. Flames blew out of the basement and up the sides of the building, entering windows on all three floors, setting multiple fires. Within moments, the fire was spreading throughout the structure.

The six people who died were all in apartments on the first floor, toward the rear. These apartments were directly above the film storage area in the basement. The coroner theorized that all the victims had died from inhaling poison gasses generated by burning film. He felt they'd suffocated before the flames reached them.

Ella Vincent, forty-two, lived in an apartment near the front of the building. Unfortunately, at the time of the fire, she was visiting Sadie Osborne, who lived in an apartment in the rear. While the two women visited, Mrs. Osborne's son, Harry Rowland, eighteen, talked to a friend on the telephone. When the explosion and fire occurred, all three fled the apartment. Mrs. Osborne escaped safely, but Harry Rowland and Ella Vincent didn't survive. Due to the smoke and confusion, the three became separated after leaving the apartment. Mrs. Vincent was found in a hallway. Because of where her body was located, officials speculated that she might have been trying to return to her own apartment. Harry Rowland's body was also found in the hallway, although a different report said his body was recovered inside his apartment. Sadie Osborne, his mother, escaped with slight injuries. As she was being treated, she pleaded with a police officer to help find her missing son. Tragically, she didn't know the young man's body was lying, covered by a sheet, just a few feet from where she was receiving first aid.

Dr. Martha Keller, seventy-four, never left her apartment. Her body was found in her medical office, part of the apartment where she also lived. She had been a physician for about thirty years.

Rose Griffin, thirty-nine, a widow, and her two children—her daughter, Leona, nineteen, and her son, Robert, seventeen—were all found in a hallway. None of them had survived. Robert's body was located close to a rear door that was locked from the outside. The door was supposed to remain unlocked until 8:00 p.m. every day. However, for some reason, the janitor had secured it early on that fateful day. Once locked, the door could not be opened from the inside. If the door had been equipped with a panic bar–type of opener, it might have saved some lives. In a tragic twist of irony, the building owner said the janitor locked the door for the apartment occupants' safety. It was secured each evening to keep unauthorized persons out of the building.

The coroner took the bodies to the city morgue. In those days, the morgue was inside the Indianapolis Police Department Headquarters at Alabama and Pearl Streets. Once again, as in previous Indianapolis disasters, the general public was allowed to view the victims' bodies.

The April 19, 1917 *Indianapolis Star* had an article about this public viewing headlined, "New Horrors of City Morgue Draw Throngs to See Bodies." The article told of people crowding the morgue throughout the night to view what the paper described as "unrecognizable masses of charred flesh." The same article described a scene in the morgue: "Two women came, bringing a very young girl with them." Spotting the trio, an observant policeman stopped them at the door and said, "Don't bring that child in here!"

The explosion broke most of Colfax Hall's windows and shattered windows in nearby structures. Then flames went up the side of the apartment building, starting numerous fires within. Other than broken windows, the exposures on the south side of Colfax Hall weren't involved in the fire.

However, flames shot across the thirty-foot-wide Pierson Street, causing several fires in the Royal Hotel on the northeast corner of Illinois and Tippecanoe Streets. The rear of that hotel was on the west side of Pierson Street. The hotel suffered an estimated $1,000 ($23,282) in damage to its windows, furniture, curtains and other furnishings in several hotel rooms.

Francis Rocket, a guest at the Royal, was lying on his stomach, relaxing on the bed in his room, which faced the Colfax building. Suddenly, he heard an explosion, and as his window shattered, he immediately felt a burning sensation. Almost instantly, the back of his clothing was on fire. Luckily, he had the presence of mind to roll over and extinguish his flaming clothes. He then ran out of his room to safety without any serious injuries.

Another guest of the hotel, Eugene Wagner, also had a narrow escape. He also had a room in the rear, across the alley from the Colfax building. He had opened his window and was sitting in a chair, just looking out and killing time. A friend stopped by, and Mr. Wagner left to walk with them. The explosion occurred less than ten minutes after he'd left his room. Later, after the fire was out, Mr. Wagner went to his room to recover his belongings. The room suffered some damage and the fire had severely burned the chair he'd been sitting in. He probably would have been seriously injured if he'd been sitting there when the explosion occurred.

Frank Wiseman, a civilian, was walking nearby when the fire broke out. He ran toward the north side of Colfax Hall, where he saw a woman and a child at a second-story window calling for help. Smoke was coming from the room behind them. Mary Springer had her four-year-old daughter in her arms, and Mr. Wiseman pleaded with her not to jump. He looked around and saw that some other people had found a stepladder, but it wasn't tall enough to reach the second-story window where the woman and child were. Thinking quickly, he had bystanders boost him high enough so that he could grab the sill of a first-floor window. The room behind that window was on fire, and as he held onto the sill, Mr. Wiseman's hand and arm suffered burns. He took the stepladder, and while holding onto the sill with his left hand, he used his right hand to lift the ladder to the second-floor window. He instructed the woman to place her young daughter on the top of the ladder with the child's back against the outside wall. Wiseman then slowly lowered the ladder with the child on top of it. When it was low enough, Wiseman tipped the ladder slightly so that the child fell safely into the outstretched arms of the crowd below. Now, it was the mother's turn, but the blaze in her room was getting hotter by the second. She was desperate to escape the heat and flames and made a frantic leap. As she jumped, Wiseman, who had dropped the stepladder, reached out with his free arm and grabbed her as she fell past him. Her momentum pulled him away from the windowsill, and they both fell into the alley. Miraculously, he had slowed her descent, so neither of them were injured by the fall. Frank Wiseman was taken to a nearby doctor's office for treatment of severe burns to his left hand and arm. Mr. Wiseman later stated, "My hand felt like I was holding onto a red-hot stove. But I would have let my arm burn off before I would let the fire burn that little girl."

Dr. Fletcher Hodges, who treated Mr. Wiseman's burns, was so impressed with the rescue that he announced that he would nominate Frank Wiseman for a Carnegie Medal for Heroism. But unfortunately, Mr. Wiseman's name does not appear on the list of people awarded this honor.

The fire department was first notified of the incident by an IFD watchman stationed in a watchtower on the roof of the Merchant's Bank building at

Meridian and Washington Streets. He heard the explosion and saw flames blowing out the windows. The first alarm was sounded at 6:48 p.m., followed by a second alarm at 6:53 p.m. Upon their arrival, firefighters found heavy smoke and fire pouring from the building. After a three-hour battle, they finally brought the fire under control. Damage was estimated at around $30,000 ($698,460).

Once the fire was out, the firefighters could thoroughly search the building. Initially, they thought there would be more victims found. However, after an extensive search, the death toll remained at six.

The Indiana state fire marshal investigated the fire. Fire Marshal H.H. Friedley had this to say: "To leave such large quantities of flammable material outside of the vault, that had been constructed as a safeguard, exposed to a spark of fire or chance ignition, was careless in the extreme, amounting to a criminal disregard of life and he [Mr. Sereinsky] should be held to account." He also chastised the owner of the building by saying, "They gave more thought to the paltry sum of rent money that they earned monthly from the chemical company than they did to the safety and welfare of their tenants and their property. That the building inspector required a vault, a fact known to the owner should have put them on guard as to the danger of the business being conducted in their basement."

A little over a week after the fire, the city building commissioner, Mr. Hilkene, drafted an ordinance to regulate the storage of movie film. This was an attempt to prevent tragedies such as this fire. The handling, manufacturing and storage of motion picture film would not be allowed in any building used for public assemblies, such as schools, churches, retail stores, hotels, apartment buildings or any building with more than a single residential unit. Movie theaters were already licensed and had their own ordinances.

On April 19, 1917, Louis Sereinsky was arrested for manslaughter in connection with the fire. He was released on a $2,500 ($59,966) bond that same afternoon. After many delays and continuances, his case finally came to trial almost two years later, in January 1919. Many witnesses were interviewed during the proceedings. The first witness was Otto Winkenhofer, an agent for a rental company. He testified that he had previously evicted Mr. Sereinsky's chemical business from one of his buildings due to the dangerous nature of the films he was storing there. Clarence Smith, the janitor at the Colfax building, testified that he frequently saw barrels and boxes of films outside the vault.

The Indiana state food and drug commissioner, Harry Barnard, testified about the dangerous chemicals found in the film. He also said that it had been known for a long time that movie and X-ray films were highly flammable and explosive.

Roy Gleason testified that he had worked for the chemical company in 1916. He said he'd been cautioned never to smoke or have any open flame while working in the basement.

Mr. Sereinsky admitted that at least fourteen barrels of films had been in the basement. However, he stated they were not in the vault because he was shipping them to another location. In his defense, he testified that he thought a natural gas explosion had caused the fire. Prosecutors then called gas company officials to testify. They stated that they had investigated the building the day after the fire and found no gas leaks in any of the gas lines within the structure. The trial lasted more than two weeks, but ultimately, Louis Sereinsky was found not guilty by the jury.

On June 10, 1919, a fire occurred on a farm about two miles south of Indianapolis. In a scenario very reminiscent of the Colfax fire, this incident also began with a large explosion quickly followed by fire. It started in a concrete building rented by Louis Sereinsky for storing motion picture film. The flames spread rapidly to other buildings. Since the farm was outside the city limits, the Indianapolis Fire Department did not respond to this incident. However, neighbors formed a bucket brigade and were able to keep the fire from spreading to the farmhouse. The fire destroyed a large barn and heavily damaged four concrete buildings that were attached to the barn. Unfortunately, sixty hogs and one hundred chickens died in the flames. The total loss was $15,000 ($349,230).

The damaged apartment building was repaired and reopened later in 1917. Indianapolis City Directories show that the Colfax Apartments underwent a name change in 1919 and became the University Park Apartments.

The entire complex and two neighboring buildings on its south side were razed in the mid-1920s. Then an eleven-story structure called the Chamber of Commerce building was constructed on the site in 1926. That historic building still stands.

ABOUT THE AUTHOR

Jack Finney has always lived in central Indiana. Born in Indianapolis, he grew up in Plainfield and has called Avon home for the last forty-five years. He retired after a career as a design draftsman. Researching the history of the Indianapolis Fire Department is a hobby of his. He also enjoys reading and has an extensive library, including over seven hundred books on firefighting, fire apparatus and fire department history. He served as a volunteer firefighter and photographer for the Wayne Township (Marion County) Fire Department for nineteen years. He was also a member of the track rescue team at the Indianapolis Motor Speedway from 1977 to 2016. He and Lesley have been married since 1970. They have two children and eight grandchildren.

Visit us at
www.historypress.com
··